# THE CARDIFF CITY MISCELLANY

## BLUEBIRDS HISTORY, TRIVIA, FACTS & STATS

# THE CARDIFF CITY MISCELLANY

## BLUEBIRDS HISTORY, TRIVIA, FACTS & STATS

## RICHARD SHEPHERD

# THE CARDIFF CITY MISCELLANY

## BLUEBIRDS HISTORY, TRIVIA, FACTS & STATS

All statistics, facts and figures are correct as of 31st July 2007

© Richard Shepherd

Richard Shepherd has asserted his rights in accordance with the Copyright, Designs and Patents Act 1988 to be identified as the author of this work.

Published By:
Pitch Publishing (Brighton) Ltd
A2 Yeoman Gate
Yeoman Way
Durrington
BN13 3QZ

Email: info@pitchpublishing.co.uk
Web: www.pitchpublishing.co.uk

First published 2007

A catalogue record for this book is available from the British Library.

10-digit ISBN: 1-9054110-4-9
13-digit ISBN: 978-1-9054110-4-7

Printed and bound in Great Britain by Cromwell Press

# FOREWORD BY BRIAN CLARK

I had two spells with Cardiff City but my first period, from 1967 to 1972, was undoubtedly the most successful time of my career. I came into what was developing into a good side in the old Second Division with players such as Don Murray, Brian Harris, Barrie Jones, Peter King, John Toshack just to name a few, and later came Bobby Woodruff and Ian Gibson. I found it easy to play alongside John Toshack, and we had some successful seasons together, getting a lot of goals between us before he joined Liverpool.

It was a good move for me coming to Cardiff after 18 months at Huddersfield Town, where things had started reasonably for me after I joined them from my hometown club Bristol City. But then an eye injury disrupted my career, and in the end I was unhappy not having a first-team place. So matters picked up for me in Cardiff with a promotion challenge and regular European football which took me all over the continent. There was that unforgettable home game with Real Madrid, in which I was lucky enough to score the goal which gave us a 1-0 first-leg win. I still think that there were more than the official 47,500 at Ninian Park on that evening in March 1971 – what a night that was and one I will remember for the rest of my life.

After my first spell at Cardiff I went to AFC Bournemouth and then Millwall, before returning to Ninian Park in 1975. My family and I have lived in Cardiff ever since, and I have always maintained my interest in City. I was not able to watch them regularly while playing for Newport County or while managing in the Welsh League – but I always kept an eye on events, and over the last eight years I have been a regular at home games as co-commentator on Cardiff City World's internet match commentary.

Stories about the club always interested me, and a particular one in this fascinating book stands out: that marathon Wartime Cup game against Bristol City at Ninian Park in April 1945. My father Don Clark played for Bristol City in that match, which under the competition's rules went on for three hours and 22 minutes until Cardiff netted the winner. Dad, who is now in his 90th year, often told me about the game and how his team had missed the last train home. They had to stay at the Angel Hotel and didn't get back until the Sunday morning. My late mother never quite believed the reason for that; she always maintained that they only stayed in Cardiff to have a night out!

Another story in this book brings back memories about *The Western Mail's* famous rugby correspondent J B G Thomas, who covered our European Cup Winners' Cup return match with PO Lanarca in Cyprus – because he was holidaying there at the time. We only drew 0-0, having beaten them 8-0 at Ninian Park. Our manager Jimmy Scoular was furious that we had strolled through the match, because a large number of British servicemen, from the army base at nearby Akrotiri, had paid good money to come and see us – so the next morning he made us train in the heat before we flew home.

I read the story about Derek Tapscott's altercation in the visitors' dressing room at Ninian Park with his former Arsenal manager George Swindin, after Tappy had scored a controversial winner for City against Arsenal in 1960. I live near Tappy and spoke to him about it; he confirmed every word!

There are a lot of great tales here about Cardiff City; Richard Shepherd has done a terrific job putting this book together. I've known him for many years, and if you want to know anything about the Bluebirds or South Wales football, he's the person to ask. I'm sure that all Cardiff City fans will enjoy reading this book.

Finally, reading that City's Colin Hudson got married in Newport on the morning of a home game against Liverpool in December 1957 got me thinking. He and his best man Alan Harrington, who was named in the team with him, rushed to Ninian Park by car from the reception. They arrived shortly before kick-off and Colin scored the opening goal in a 6-1 win. Now if any of the players had said to Jimmy Scoular that we were getting married on the morning of a game and that we would be there just before kick-off, I can just imagine what his reaction would have been!

*Brian Clark, Cardiff City 1967-72 and 1975-76*

# INTRODUCTION

It was twenty years ago when I found that my connections with Cardiff City went back much further than the particular date of 2 April 1956, which was the very first time that I saw the club in action. That day, they lost 3-2 at home to Portsmouth in the original First Division, and I have seen them play during every successive season from then up to the present day. Anything that had happened before that Portsmouth match was something that I had yet to discover at that time.

One of my discoveries came through a relative, who sent me a family tree that included Cardiff-born Sol Shepherd, a cousin of my grandfather. My relative revealed that Sol had been a close acquaintance of Bartley Wilson, the founder of Cardiff City. Sol had played for City when they were an amateur club before turning professional in 1910 – in fact, he appeared in a 1909/10 team-photograph, so my family links with the club span nearly one hundred years. My father first watched City in August 1921 as a nine year-old, and was a season-ticket holder, together with my uncle, from the end of the Second World War up to the late 1950s.

In 1967, I came across a Cardiff City match programme for their FA Cup tie against Tottenham Hotspur at Ninian Park in February 1923. My curiosity about this game got the better of me, and I found the result, match report, line-ups and so on in the local reference library by looking up the *Western Mail* edition for that particular weekend. That led to a weekly visit to the library, and over the next few years, I researched all of City's Southern League, Football League and Cup matches, transfers in and out, and any matters of interest connected with the club.

That research was completed in 1970, and from then on it was a case of keeping a season-by-season diary. That is still ongoing, and is contained in a ledger that is the basis for *The Cardiff City Miscellany*. I have also made use of the *Definitive Cardiff City*, together with various other publications covering the club, as well as match programmes from 1910 to the present day. The unique collection of bound volumes from 1913 to 1932, produced by Cardiff City director Walter Parker in his role as programme-editor and managing director of the club's printers for many years, has been a valuable source of information. Walter Parker would hardly have believed that decades later, his informative writing about the club's activities would be used to show present-day fans what life was like around Cardiff City in those days. Likewise, succeeding editors would also leave on record details of the club's behind the scenes activities of later years.

In the past 51 years, I have been connected with Cardiff City as a spectator, radio and television reporter, commentator, and match programme editor. For the past few years, I have been part of the club's media department, being involved in the match magazine as well as being the club's internet commentator on Cardiff City World. Over the years, I have also become the club's archivist, and as such have been in an ideal position to compile *The Cardiff City Miscellany*.

*Richard Shepherd – June 2007*

## FORMER RUBBISH TIP AND LORD NINIAN

In 1910, Bluebirds founder Bartley Wilson and director Ivor Parker, one of Wilson's original players with Riverside FC, later to become Cardiff City, were seeking a suitable site on which to build an enclosed ground. This followed the decision of the amateur Cardiff City to turn professional and compete in the Second Division of the Southern League. They were advised by Councillor John Mander to look at a piece of waste ground off Sloper Road, commonly known as Tanyard Lane, with a view to leasing several acres in order to build their ground. The whole area had formed part of the Corporation refuse tip, and was being used as allotments. They eventually chose five acres a few hundred yards from the junction with Leckwith Road. They duly leased the land, and built a primitive ground to hold about 10,000 spectators on ash-banks built up with refuse, slag from factory furnaces, and anything else they could lay their hands on. The new stadium was named Ninian Park after Lord Ninian Crichton-Stuart, younger son of the Third Marquis of Bute, who had come in as a guarantor of the annual rent when the club urgently needed to complete the required numbers of guarantors in order to secure their lease. Lord Ninian was killed in action at the Battle of Loos in Belgium during October 1915.

## INTERNATIONAL SCORING DEBUT

Long-serving Cardiff City defender Phil Dwyer marked his Welsh international debut on 18 April 1978 by scoring the winner when Wales defeated Iran 1-0 in Tehran. He also had a goal disallowed, and hit the post with another effort.

## TRIO OF BROTHERS

In the late 1940s and early 1950s, the three Cardiff-born Stitfall brothers – Ron, Albert and Bob – were all on Cardiff City's playing staff. Full-back Ron, who also played on occasion in attack, and winger Albert were in the first team together on several occasions. Goalkeeper Bob never played a first-team game, but all three were together a number of times in the reserves.

## A LONG TRIP HOME

After a 1-0 win at Sunderland in the FA Cup first (now third) round on 8 January 1921, the Bluebirds took twelve hours to get back from the north-east to Cardiff by train. They left Sunderland at 6pm, changed at Newcastle, and did not arrive back in South Wales until 6am on Sunday.

## FAMOUS NAMES

Ninian Park has, over the years, seen some famous names visit the ground. In March 1945 Mrs Clementine Churchill, wife of the Prime Minister, attended the regional League West match against Swansea Town to publicise the City of Cardiff YWCA appeal. Churchill himself was at Ninian Park in February 1950, then being the Leader of the Tory Opposition. His visit was for a political rally held at the ground prior to the following month's General Election. On 31 October 1953, Field Marshal Viscount Montgomery of Alamein, who was in Cardiff on military ceremonial duty, attended the Cardiff City v Charlton Athletic match. Labour Party Leader Hugh Gaitskell saw the Cardiff City v Ipswich Town game on 25 November 1961. James Callaghan (eventually Prime Minister and later Lord Callaghan) who was MP for Cardiff South, the constituency in which Ninian Park was situated, attended matches on several occasions in the 1960s and 1970s. The Pope attended a religious rally in June 1982. And a regular spectator at Ninian Park is ex-Labour Party Leader and former European Commissioner Neil (now Lord) Kinnock, a Bluebirds supporter for over 50 years.

## THE DRINKS ARE ON US

When Cardiff City were in Switzerland during May 1960 following the club's promotion to Division One, the players decided that they would buy drinks for the directors by way of thanks for the trip abroad. Bluebirds forward Derek Tapscott, who was in the chair, ordered what the directors wanted, as well as drinks for all the players – and put the lot on the club's bill! None of the directors complained.

## THE WEEKEND WAR BROKE OUT

The Third Division (South) home match on 2 September 1939 against Notts County was something of an unreal event for the 20,000 Bluebirds fans who watched City lose 2-4 at Ninian Park. The international political situation was so grave that everyone was expecting war to break out between Britain and Germany at any moment. It happened the next morning, when Prime Minister Neville Chamberlain announced to the nation that the two countries were indeed now at war. City's players came in on the Monday morning to find that their contracts had been terminated, as was the case with every other League club, and League football was suspended for the duration. The Bluebirds were back in action in mid-September for a month of hurriedly-arranged friendly matches before regional League competitions began.

## PRAISE FROM A FAMOUS JOURNALIST

One of the best-known football journalists in the early part of the twentieth century was the editor of the weekly *Athletic News* – J A H Catton, who wrote under the name of Tityrus. In October 1920, he paid a well-deserved compliment to both the directors and players of Cardiff City after the first couple of months of the Bluebirds' first-ever League season: 'I am told that there is a notice in the home dressing-room of Cardiff City requesting the players to observe the laws of the game, and not to question the decisions of the referee. An official who took charge of two important City games up to that time was agreeably surprised by the behaviour of the team that relied on legitimate and fair football. That is the spirit of a team and it will pay.'

## CAREER-ENDING INJURY

Devon-born goalkeeper Phil Joslin, who joined Cardiff City from Torquay United in the summer of 1948, had his career ended by a broken leg in August 1951. It occurred in a pre-season public-practice match (blues v whites) when he collided with centre-forward Wilf Grant. Joslin never played again.

## CHARITY SHIELD SUCCESS

Following their FA Cup Final victory over Arsenal in 1927, Cardiff City were invited by the Football Association to play in the FA Charity Shield (now the Community Shield) against the famous amateur side Corinthians. Their line-up included several top amateurs who had played for the full England side, leading amateurs in those days being equal to the standard of top professionals. The game took place at Chelsea on 12 October 1927, and City beat Corinthians 2-1. The Bluebirds were therefore holders of the FA Cup, the Welsh Cup and the Charity Shield.

## BLUE IS THE COLOUR

Cardiff City have always played in blue shirts as their first-choice colours since officially adopting their name in 1908 as an amateur club, two years before turning professional in 1910. The pattern of the colours has altered over the years, as have the various trims, sometimes with white sleeves, and in several periods all blue:

| *Date* | *Shirt/shorts* |
| --- | --- |
| September 1910 to April 1935 | Blue/white |
| August 1935 to April 1942 | Blue with white sleeves/white |
| August 1942 to June 1947 | Blue/white |
| August 1947 to May 1949 | Blue with white sleeves/white |
| August 1949 to May 1954 | Blue/white |
| August 1954 to November 1955 | Blue with white sleeves/white |
| November 1955 to September 1965 | Blue/white |
| September 1965 to September 1967 | All blue |
| September 1967 to May 1975 | Blue/white |
| August 1975 to May 1982 | All blue |
| August 1982 to May 1995 | Blue/white |
| August 1995 to May 1996 | All blue |
| August 1996 to May 1998 | Blue/white |
| August 1998 to May 1999 | Blue with white sleeves/white |
| August 1999 to May 2000 | Blue/white |
| August 2000 to May 2007 | All blue |
| August 2007 to present | Blue/white |

## PLAYERS AS BUILDERS

Ninian Park was officially opened on 1 September 1910, with a friendly match against an Aston Villa side consisting of first team and reserve players. The new ground had a canvas-roofed stand on the Sloper Road side holding 200 seated spectators. In November 1910 a more substantial timber stand, holding nearly 3000 tightly-packed seated fans, was built along two-thirds of the pitch from the Canton End. Several skilled carpenters were used, helped by City's players, who worked as labourers to supplement their club wages. The communal dressing room, used by both home and visiting teams, was in a wooden chalet-style building in the Sloper Road/Canton End corner. The new stand was extended along the length of the pitch in 1913 following City's promotion to the First Division of the Southern League, and new dressing rooms were built under it in 1919.

## THREE UP, BUT LOST!

In their Welsh Cup fifth round replay at Ninian Park on 8 February 1966, City were leading 3-0 in the second half when defender Don Murray was sent off by Merthyr referee Leo Callaghan for allegedly head-butting Swansea's Jimmy McLaughlin, though to this day Murray still denies that he made contact. Ten-man City collapsed, and Swansea took the game into extra time at 3-3 before going on to win 5-3.

## TWO GREAT BLUEBIRD NAMES

Two legendary Cardiff City figures passed away in 1954. Former secretary/manager Fred Stewart, who served the club for 22 years from 1911 to 1933, died at the age of 81 on 11 February. And club founder and former assistant secretary Bartley Wilson, who had been manager in 1933/34, died at the age of 84 on 19 November. Wilson had been associated with the club from its formation by him as Riverside in the autumn of 1899 until his retirement from Cardiff City's administrative staff in mid-May 1954, a spell of almost 55 years.

## AN INTERNATIONAL DRESSING ROOM

Between 24 October and 20 November 1925, there were a record number of 16 internationals (current or capped within the previous two years) on Cardiff City's staff. They were Harry Beadles (Wales), Jimmy Blair (Scotland), Joe Cassidy (Scotland), Len Davies (Wales), Billy Davies (Wales), Herbie Evans (Wales), Jack Evans (Wales), Tom Farquharson (Ireland), Fred Keenor (Wales), Denis Lawson (Scotland), Jack Lewis (Wales), Pat McIlvenny (Ireland), Jimmy Nelson (Scotland), Jack Nicholas (Wales), Tommy Sloan (Ireland), and Edgar Thomas (Wales). Furthermore, Tommy Watson gained his first cap for Ireland in February 1926.

## A COWSHED DRESSING ROOM

When Cardiff City played at Cwm Albion in the Glamorgan League on 26 September 1910, their changing facilities were somewhat primitive. The home side changed in a comfortable room at a local pub near the ground. But City, who lost 1-0, had to get ready near to the ground in a disused cowshed that passed for the visitors' dressing room!

## THE MARATHON JOURNEY

Cardiff City's European Cup Winners' Cup quarter-final second-leg match against Moscow Torpedo on 19 March 1968 involved an 8000-mile round trip. The game was staged in the Asian city of Tashkent because Moscow was in its icebound mid-winter at the time. In order to get to Tashkent in time for the game, City brought forward their Second Division away match against Middlesbrough from 16 March to 9 March, as both clubs had a spare date on what was FA Cup fifth round day. Several days later, the Bluebirds set off, stopping for two days in Moscow before heading off to Tashkent. After a 1-0 defeat, which meant a play-off at Augsburg in West Germany, City took 26 hours to get back to Cardiff, arriving home in the early hours of Thursday morning. They then had to play Hull City at Ninian Park 36 hours after their return – and the Bluebirds lost 3-2.

## LATHAM'S GOOD DEED

Cardiff City's long-serving trainer George Latham never forgot his roots in Newtown, Mid Wales. His mother had been a nurse at the Montgomeryshire County Hospital in Newtown, and at the end of most seasons in the 1920s, Latham would take City to play a friendly against Montgomeryshire at Newtown in order to raise much-needed funds for the Hospital. So the Bluebirds turned out against the amateurs in May 1923, May 1925, May 1927, May 1928, and May 1929, while in May 1930 they played West Bromwich Albion there for the same cause. Latham was a highly-respected trainer/masseur in Football and often treated players from other sports. In the summer of 1924, he was invited by the British Olympic Association to travel to Paris for the Olympic Games of that year to act as masseur to the British team. They gave him a special commemorative medal in appreciation of his services.

## QUICK OFF THE MARK

The fastest goal ever recorded for Cardiff City was by Welsh international centre-forward Trevor Ford at Charlton on 23 October 1954: Ford scored just fifteen seconds from the kick-off. It was, however, a false dawn – City lost 4-1!

## LYN'S 32-GOAL NIGHTMARE

Cardiff City goalkeeper Lyn Davies, a former apprentice, was a highly-rated young player with the club - but he had a disastrous month during 1966/67. Coming into the side for the Second Division game at Wolverhampton Wanderers on 21 September, he was on the wrong end of a 7-1 defeat! His next four matches saw City lose 5-0 at Charlton, draw 1-1 at home to Derby, lose 4-2 at home to Hull, and then lose 7-1 at Plymouth on 15 October. During that spell, he made his only Wales under-23 appearance, at Wolverhampton against England, who put eight past him – a total of 32 goals conceded by Davies in six matches. To be fair to the keeper, he stood little chance with most of them because of poor defending.

## HIGHS AND LOWS

Cardiff City's lowest-ever average home league attendance over one season was 2856 in 1986/87, when the club had dropped into Division Four. During that season, City had their lowest-ever league attendance since entering the Football League in 1920 – 1510 for the visit of Hartlepool United on 7 May 1987. The club's highest average home league attendance was in season 1952/53 – 37,937.

## ABANDONED MATCHES

Only three league matches at Ninian Park have been abandoned during play since Cardiff City entered the Football League in 1920. On Boxing Day 1946, the Third Division (South) game with Leyton Orient, being watched by 35,000, was called off at 0-0 near the end of the first half because of pitch conditions. On 13 March 1963, the Second Division match against Plymouth Argyle, attended by 8999 spectators, was halted at 1-1 after 53 minutes because of heavy rain. And on 4 November 1967, the Division Two game with Millwall ended at 0-0 after 31 minutes in front of 7717 because torrential pre-match rain had left the pitch waterlogged.

## BOXING OCCASIONS

On 15 June 1967, Ninian Park staged the World Featherweight Championship title fight between challenger Howard Winstone of Merthyr and holder Vicente Saldivar of Mexico. Winstone was meeting Saldivar for the second time, having previously lost to him at London's Earls Court in September 1965. An attendance of 42,000 saw the Ninian Park contest, in which Winstone was controversially defeated on points over fifteen rounds. It was not the first time that professional boxing had been held at the ground. On 3 February 1932, Cardiff-born Jack Petersen had fought Dick Power for the Welsh Heavyweight Title, winning by a first-round knock-out. And Ronnie James from Swansea had challenged American Ike Williams at Ninian Park on 4 September 1946 for the World Lightweight Title, when 45,000 watched James knocked out in the ninth round.

## HAPPY DAYS ARE HERE AGAIN!

St Saviour's Silver Band was the regular pre-match and half-time entertainment at Ninian Park from 1919 to 1939. They would play popular numbers of the day, and in the early 1930s decided to use a new American song – 'Happy Days Are Here Again'. It had been composed following the 1932 election of United States President Franklin D Roosevelt who had promised his country a 'new deal' to counter its economic depression. So in 1933/34, Cardiff City ran out regularly to 'Happy Days Are Here Again'... only to finish bottom of Division Three (South), forcing them to seek re-election to the Football League.

## DOUBLE PROMOTION

Only two managers in Cardiff City's history have taken the club to promotion on two separate occasions. Fred Stewart took City up as Champions of the Southern League Second Division in 1912/13, and as runners-up in the Football League's Second Division in 1920/21. Frank Burrows led the club to promotion from Division Four in 1987/88, and in his second spell with the club took City up from Division Three to Division Two in 1998/99.

## RECORD APPEARANCE HOLDER

Grangetown-born Phil Dwyer holds the all-time appearance record for Cardiff City. A Welsh Schools international, he joined the club as an apprentice in 1969 at the age of 16. He made his first-team debut at right-back against Leyton Orient at Brisbane Road on 7 October 1972 in a 0-0 draw. During his career he appeared in defence, midfield and attack, playing a total of 471 League games for the club, 28 League Cup matches, 23 FA Cup ties, 43 Welsh Cup games, and 5 European Cup Winners' Cup fixtures. In total he played 573 senior games for the club. His final appearance for City was in a 4-1 home defeat by Notts County on 17 March 1985. He then joined Rochdale, with whom he ended his League career that season. Phil also played for Wales at under-23, under-21 and senior level (ten appearances).

# CARDIFF CITY MANAGERS

| Manager | From | To |
|---|---|---|
| Davy McDougall | August 1910 | April 1911 |
| Fred Stewart | May 1911 | May 1933 |
| Bartley Wilson | May 1933 | February 1934 |
| Ben Watts-Jones | February 1934 | April 1937 |
| Bill Jennings | April 1937 | April 1939 |
| Cyril Spiers | April 1939 | June 1946 |
| Billy McCandless | June 1946 | November 1947 |
| Cyril Spiers | December 1947 | May 1954 |
| Trevor Morris | May 1954 | July 1958 |
| Bill Jones | September 1958 | September 1962 |
| George Swindin | November 1962 | April 1964 |
| Jimmy Scoular | June 1964 | November 1973 |
| Frank O'Farrell | November 1973 | April 1974 |
| Jimmy Andrews | May 1974 | November 1978 |
| Richie Morgan | November 1978 | November 1981 |
| Graham Williams | November 1981 | February 1982 |
| Len Ashurst | March 1982 | March 1984 |
| Jimmy Goodfellow | March 1984 | September 1984 |
| Alan Durban | September 1984 | May 1986 |
| Frank Burrows | May 1986 | August 1989 |
| Len Ashurst | August 1989 | May 1991 |
| Eddie May | July 1991 | November 1994 |
| Terry Yorath | November 1994 | March 1995 |
| Eddie May | March 1995 | May 1995 |
| Kenny Hibbitt | July 1995 | January 1996 |
| Phil Neal | January 1996 | October 1996 |
| Russell Osman | November 1996 | December 1996 |
| Kenny Hibbitt | December 1996 | February 1998 |
| Frank Burrows | February 1998 | January 2000 |
| Billy Ayre | February 2000 | August 2000 |
| Bobby Gould | August 2000 | October 2000 |
| Alan Cork | October 2000 | February 2002 |
| Lennie Lawrence | February 2002 | May 2005 |
| Dave Jones | May 2005 | |

## TAXI MISHAP

When, on 28 March 1925, Cardiff City returned home by train after their 3-1 FA Cup semi-final win against Blackburn Rovers at Notts County's Meadow Lane, there was a large crowd to meet them at Cardiff General Station. One of City's goalscorers – Joe Nicholson – tried to escape from over-enthusiastic fans by climbing onto the canvas roof of a taxi. He fell through it, injured his knee, and was forced to miss the next two League games.

## CHARLIE'S MARATHON WALK

Bluebirds' supporter Charlie Manley of Gray Street, Cardiff, was such a keen City fan that he decided to walk to Chelsea for the game at Stamford Bridge on 25 February 1922. Accompanied by a colleague, he made fairly good time despite being delayed by his friend who could not walk as fast. After walking back to Cardiff following City's 1-0 defeat, Charlie decided to walk to Newcastle and then Liverpool to watch Cardiff City in two of their away games during April 1922. So the former World War One soldier, who was unemployed, left Cardiff at 6am on Tuesday, March 21st and walked via Shrewsbury, Manchester, Leeds and York. He struggled through a heavy snowstorm, the last 48 miles from Northallerton in Yorkshire taking 14 hours, and arrived in Newcastle on Friday 31 March, the day before the game. His 350-mile walk took him nine-and-a-half-days, and his average daily distance was 35 miles. Following City's 0-0 draw at St James Park, he set off at noon on the Sunday to walk to Liverpool for the Bluebirds' game at Anfield on April 15th. He arrived well in time to see City's 5-1 defeat by the eventual League Champions, and then set off for home after the match. By the time he reached Leominster, he had done enough, and travelled the rest of the way by train, arriving in Cardiff on the night of Sunday 16th April. Charlie had walked a total of 650 miles, and worn out two pairs of boots and four pairs of socks. He had been away for 26 days, sometimes sleeping rough, occasionally being taken in for the night by sympathetic onlookers. At least he didn't have to pay to watch City's matches, being given a ticket by the players.

## A SPORTING GESTURE

Cardiff City became the first South Wales club to hold the Welsh Cup when they won it in 1911/12. They defeated Pontypridd 3-0 in a replay at Aberdare after a 0-0 draw at Ninian Park. Player/Trainer George Latham, a Welsh international who had joined the club from Stoke in February 1911, played in the replay when he came in for the injured Bob Lawrie, who was forced to miss the game. After City's win, Latham gave his Cup Winners' medal to Lawrie.

## BACK TO SQUARE ONE

The Cardiff-Arsenal FA Cup Final of 1927 was the first to be publicly broadcast on national radio by the BBC. A year earlier, the Bolton v Manchester City Final had been heard on a closed circuit at a couple of venues in Manchester and Bolton. The commentator for that 1927 Final was journalist George Allison, an Arsenal director who became their secretary/manager in 1934 on the death of Herbert Chapman. Allison had an assistant with his commentary whose role was to refer to a *Radio Times* diagram of eight squares of the pitch. The assistant would call out the number of the square in which the ball then was – the origin of the phrase "back to square one".

## ATHLETIC CITY BOSS

On 2 May 1980, Aberdare-born Ron Jones was appointed Cardiff City's General Manager, and later became the club's managing director/secretary. He had spent the previous four years in a commercial role with Queens Park Rangers. Jones had been one of Britain's outstanding sprinters in an athletics career that included captaining the British Olympic team at the 1968 Mexico Games. He competed for Wales in four Commonwealth Games – Cardiff (1958), Perth (1962), Jamaica (1966) and Edinburgh (1970). At the time of his Bluebirds' appointment, he was still the Welsh record holder for the 100 and 200 metres. He remained with Cardiff City until May 1988, when he resigned to join Portsmouth under his former QPR chairman Jim Gregory.

## NO HIT FOR KEENOR

In October 1919, legendary Cardiff boxer 'Peerless' Jim Driscoll, the former World Featherweight Champion, was in training at Ninian Park for the final contest of his career against Frenchman Charles Ledoux. 39-year-old Driscoll, a Bluebirds fan, was returning to the ring after a long absence, and during his training sessions sparred with Cardiff City's Fred Keenor for a couple of rounds. Despite the 14-year difference in their ages, Keenor never managed to lay a glove on the veteran boxer. Driscoll lost to Ledoux at the National Sporting Club in London on 20 October 1919, being stopped in the 16th round of the 20-round contest. Peerless Jim, a well-respected and popular sporting figure in Cardiff, continued to be a supporter of the Bluebirds, and when he died at the end of January 1925 at the premature age of 45, City's players and officials were amongst the estimated 100,000 who attended his Cardiff funeral.

## TWO PENALTIES, TWO MISSES!

In 1959/60, the Bluebirds had clinched promotion to Division One on 16 April with a 1-0 win over already-promoted Aston Villa, which moved them into top place. A win over struggling Plymouth Argyle three days later would have put City within sight of the Second Division title. They had not been awarded a penalty all season, but against Plymouth they had two – and missed them both! Brian Walsh shot wide in the first half, and Danny Malloy's second-half effort was saved. Argyle's 1-0 win confirmed their Second Division safety, while City ended the season one point behind title-winners Villa. A win over Argyle would have meant City finishing in top place.

## LONG RUN

Between 26 October 1968 and September 1971, full-back David Carver did not miss a League or Cup match for Cardiff City, playing in 154 consecutive matches. He joined the Bluebirds from Rotherham United in January 1966 and left for Hereford United in August 1973.

## BUSY FIRST SEASON

Cardiff City took part in the Second Division of the Southern League in their first season – 1910/11 – as a professional club. But the division contained only twelve clubs, five of them from South Wales, giving an inadequate 22-match programme. So the Bluebirds also played their first team in the Glamorgan League, giving them another eighteen matches, as that competition contained ten South Wales clubs. City supplemented their season with thirteen friendly matches, and also played in the FA Cup (two qualifying matches) and the Welsh Cup (four matches) – a total of 59 games in that first season of professionalism.

## WHERE'S THE MONEY GONE?

Following a 0-0 draw against Queens Park Rangers in an FA Cup third round tie at Ninian Park on 6 January 1990, the cash takings of £50,000 from the 13,834 attendance were left overnight in the club's office safe. The key to the safe was left in a key cupboard on a hook labelled 'safe'. The following day, it was discovered that all the cash had been stolen. It was clearly a job assisted by inside knowledge. Police enquiries revealed that two persons had known of the money from talking to matchday employees. The cash was all recovered, some of it strewn on the ground behind the Canton Stand, some of it in the house of one of the culprits, and the majority of it buried on Caerphilly mountain!

## TRIPLE CUP EXIT

At the start of February 1966, Cardiff City were still in three Cup competitions – the League Cup, the FA Cup, and the Welsh Cup. A fortnight later, the Bluebirds were out of each competition after three consecutive defeats. On 2 February they lost 5-1 at home to West Ham United, going out of the League Cup semi-final on a two-leg 3-10 aggregate. On 8 February they lost 3-5 to Swansea Town at Ninian Park in a Welsh Cup fifth round replay. Finally, they lost 0-2 at Southport in the fourth round of the FA Cup on 12 February – three Cup exits in ten days!

## PRISONERS OF WAR

Four Cardiff City players were captured by the Japanese in 1942 whilst serving in the Far East during the Second World War. They were with British forces on the island of Java when it fell. Winger Billy Baker, forwards Bobby Tobin and Billy James, and goalkeeper Jackie Pritchard were all prisoners-of-war, along with former City amateur Wilf Wooller and ex-Bluebird Ernie Curtis. Sadly, Pritchard was drowned at sea when the Japanese transport ship on which he was being taken to a POW camp, was torpedoed and sunk by an American submarine in November 1943. The other three remained in captivity for the duration, and all returned to play for City after the War.

## MERRETT PLAYED AT NINIAN PARK

Cardiff City staged the Cardiff Docks Cup Final on 27 April 1922 between two well-known firms – Watts-Coryians (a combination of Watts, Watts & Co and John Cory & Sons) played Aberdare House, the team representing Messrs. Llewellyn, Merrett & Price. Playing in the Aberdare House side was 35-year-old Herbert Merrett, a director of the firm. Seventeen years later, he joined the Cardiff City board and became chairman of the club. He was at various times a director, chairman and president of the Bluebirds until his death at the age of 72 in October 1959.

## CROWD BROKE IN!

Newly-promoted Cardiff City opened their first-ever season at top level (Division One) with a home game against the FA Cup holders Tottenham Hotspur on 27 August 1921. Three hours before the 3pm kick-off, queues stretched from the ground along Sloper Road to Leckwith Road and Wellington Street, and in the opposite direction past Ninian Park School near Virgil Street to Penarth Road. The turnstiles were shut on just over 50,000, but those left outside forced open the exit gates to gain admission. The actual attendance was never ascertained, but was thought to have been between 56,000 and 60,000!

## BLUEBIRDS CAREER

| *League and division* | *Period* |
| --- | --- |
| Southern League Division Two | 1910/11-1912/13 |
| Southern League Division One | 1913/14-1919/20 |
| Football League Division Two | 1920/21 |
| Football League Division One | 1921/22-1928/29 |
| Football League Division Two | 1929/30-1930/31 |
| Football League Division Three South | 1931/32-1946/47 |
| Football League Division Two | 1947/48-1951/52 |
| Football League Division One | 1952/53-1956/57 |
| Football League Division Two | 1957/58-1959/60 |
| Football League Division One | 1960/61-1961/62 |
| Football League Division Two | 1962/63-1974/75 |
| Football League Division Three | 1975/76 |
| Football League Division Two | 1976/77-1981/82 |
| Football League Division Three | 1982/83 |
| Football League Division Two | 1983/84-1984/85 |
| Football League Division Three | 1985/86 |
| Football League Division Four | 1986/87-1987/88 |
| Football League Division Three | 1988/89-1989/90 |
| Football League Division Four | 1990/91-1992/93* |
| Football League Division Two | 1993/94-1994/95 |
| Football League Division Three | 1995/96-1998/99 |
| Football League Division Two | 1999/2000 |
| Football League Division Three | 2000/01 |
| Football League Division Two | 2001/02-2002/03 |
| Football League Division One | 2003/04-2004/05* |
| Coca-Cola Championship | 2005/06- |

*\* Denotes seasons at the end of which the divisions were retitled*

## £450 LOSS

At the end of 1910/11, Cardiff City's first professional season, the club showed a loss of £450. The income was £1968, while the expenditure was £2418, including £1360 paid out in wages, £50 in transfer fees, and £57 for playing kit.

## MANAGER AND BUSINESSMAN

Fred Stewart was a busy man during his 22-year reign as Cardiff City's manager. In his time with the club, he was also a coal merchant and ran a corn-and-seed business, adverts for these enterprises appearing regularly in club's match programme. It was not until after his retirement as manager in May 1933 that City's registered office was moved to Ninian Park. Prior to that, it had been at Fred Stewart's various Cardiff homes in Pentre Street, Partridge Road and Newport Road.

## NAME CHANGES

The club was originally founded in 1899 as Riverside FC. Three years later, they became Riverside Albion after combining with another local club. Following the granting of city status to Cardiff in 1905, the amateur Riverside Albion began calling itself Cardiff City, much to the displeasure of the South Wales and Monmouthshire Football Association, who felt that the club was assuming an unwarranted importance. Despite several applications by secretary Bartley Wilson officially to become Cardiff City, permission was refused, though Wilson still kept using the title. But in 1908, the club was elected to the South Wales Amateur League, and official permission was given to use the name Cardiff City – on condition that if a professional club were ever formed in the city, then that new club would be entitled to use the name. In 1910, it was Wilson's amateur Cardiff City that turned professional, and therefore retained the name.

## CITY'S FIRST-EVER DISMISSAL

In the last few minutes of the game against Manchester City at Maine Road on the opening day of the 1925/26 season, with the scores level at 2-2, Cardiff's Scottish international full-back Jimmy Nelson was badly fouled in his own penalty area. The referee saw his retaliation and he was sent off – the first-ever Cardiff City player to be dismissed in a League game. A penalty was awarded to Manchester City; they scored from it, and won 3-2. Nelson was suspended for one month without pay, during which he missed five First Division games.

## THREE SENT OFF, ONE ARRESTED!

Just before the end of Cardiff City's 2-0 defeat by Crystal Palace at Selhurst Park on 31 March 1979, Palace's Dave Swindlehurst and City's Keith Pontin were involved in a scuffle after Swindlehurst had fouled Pontin. Both players were sent off by the referee, and when Phil Dwyer raced 30 yards to express his opinion about the matter to the official, he too was shown a red card. In addition, City's suspended midfielder John Buchanan, who was watching from the stand, attempted to get onto the pitch to add his views. He was intercepted by police and stewards, and 'escorted' to the detention-room, from which he was rescued after the game by manager Richie Morgan.

## GILL AND IREMONGER

Sheffield Wednesday's Jimmy Gill was Cardiff City's first signing after the Bluebirds were elected to the Football League in May 1920. The highly-talented Gill was often a humorist on the pitch, and when he scored against the notoriously short-tempered Notts County goalkeeper Albert Iremonger at Ninian Park in a 1-1 draw on 30 October 1920, he made a facetious remark, knowing that Iremonger would react. The tall Notts County goalkeeper then chased Gill to the halfway line, and would have taken the matter further, but the referee and Iremonger's team-mates persuaded him to return to his goal, and Gill kept out of his way for the rest of the game!

## ARISTOCRATIC SUPPORT

At the start of Cardiff City as a professional organisation in 1910, two of the aristocracy with Cardiff connections were associated with the club. In addition to Lord Ninian Crichton-Stuart, youngest son of the Third Marquis of Bute and one of the guarantors of the club's lease from the City Corporation, the President of the Bluebirds was the Right Honourable The Earl of Plymouth who resided at St Fagan's Castle. He retained the position until the end of the Second World War, while the noble lord died in action during World War One.

## FOOTBALLER/ACCOUNTANT

Brian Walsh, signed by Cardiff City from Arsenal in September 1955, was an outstanding winger with the Bluebirds during his six-year spell at Ninian Park, which ended in November 1961 when he joined Newport County. During his time with City, he had an eye to his future, and while his team-mates played cards on away trips, Walsh would be studying his books for his accountancy exams. He duly qualified as a Chartered Accountant during his Bluebirds career, and was often of assistance to his City colleagues in financial matters.

## PRESS MOVES

Journalists have operated from a number of various positions around Ninian Park over the years. In the first decade of the ground's existence (1910-20) they were seated in the front of the original wooden stand before moving to the gabled section on the roof. In the late 1930s, they were shifted to a wooden cabin on brick pillars in the Grange End/Sloper Road corner of the ground until the summer of 1960, when a special area was built for them in front of the main stand, which then consisted of a centre section. In 1973, journalists and media were moved to the rear of the newly extended main stand, but in the summer of 2003 they were relocated to their current position at the rear lower enclosure in the main stand.

## PLAYER, COACH, MANAGER, HOTELIER AND GROCER

Bluebirds stalwart Billy Hardy spent 21 years as a player with Cardiff City (1911-32). But what became of the bald-headed wing-half, who played in City's 1925 and 1927 FA Cup Finals? In the summer of 1932, he joined Bradford Park Avenue as coach, becoming their manager at the end of March 1934. He left them in April 1936, and ran the Dolphin Hotel at Wincanton in Somerset. In 1949 he emigrated to Hobart in Tasmania, where he and his wife Olive, a sister of former City player Charlie Pinch, ran a grocery store. They returned to Cardiff in February 1963, and eventually moved to Teignmouth in Devon. Hardy died in Iver, Buckinghamshire, at the age of 89 in March 1981.

## YOU SCRATCH MY BACK...

In the immediate post-World War Two period, Cardiff City chairman H H (later Sir Herbert) Merrett would spend his summer holidays at a Torquay hotel owned by Torquay United's chairman. With their shared interest in football, the two became friends and an arrangement was made between them. If City had any players whom they considered not quite good enough for the first team, then Torquay would be offered their services. And if the Devon club had any players who looked promising enough to make the grade in the higher divisions, then City would be offered first chance to sign them. Three players who were amongst those that made the move to Ninian Park were goalkeeper Phil Joslin, winger Mike Tiddy and forward Tommy Northcott. But the arrangement came to an acrimonious end. Cardiff-born full-back Harry Parfitt had been transferred to Torquay on the understanding that City could have him back when required. After two seasons in Devon, Parfitt was wanted back at Ninian Park in January 1954. Torquay demanded a fee of £5000 for his transfer but City offered £2500. There was a disagreement amongst the Torquay board, their president and chairman wanting to help City while the others wanted a high fee for the player. City reluctantly had to pay the full fee being asked, and as a result broke off friendly relations with Torquay – so Sir Herbert Merrett had to find another hotel!

## CRICKETING BLUEBIRDS

Five Cardiff City players have been on the books of County Cricket clubs. Forward Len Davies (1919-31) was on Glamorgan's staff when they entered the County Championship in 1921, though he did not play any first-team matches. Goalkeeper Joe Hills (1924-26) played for Kent and Glamorgan, and later became a first-class umpire. Inside-forward Ernie Carless (1932/33, 1944-46) played for Glamorgan, as well as Devon in the Minor Counties. Defender Stan Montgomery (1948-55) played for Essex and Glamorgan. Goalkeeper Ron Nicholls (1958-61) was an opening batsman for Gloucestershire, scoring 23,612 runs in a long County career. In 1966, his benefit season, he scored a century against Berkshire in the Gillette Cup.

## VALUE FOR MONEY?

Cardiff City's inside-forward or winger John McSeveney, whom they signed from Sunderland in the summer of 1955, was transferred to Newport County in July 1957. At the time, McSeveney and his family were occupying a Cardiff City club house in Solva Avenue, Llanishen, and the player did not want to move from there. So Newport bought McSeveney and the house in a package deal. Years later, McSeveney revealed that Newport had paid more for the house than they did for him!

## THREE OPENING GOALS, THREE DIFFERENT CLUBS

Southend-born forward Frank Dudley had a remarkable record in the 1953/54 season, when his first three goals of that season were scored for three different clubs. Having played for Southend United and Leeds United, he joined Southampton in 1951. During 53/54, he scored several goals for the Saints before moving to the Bluebirds in mid-October. His first and only goal for City was in a 5-0 home win over Charlton on 31 October 1953, and his next goal was for Brentford, whom he joined in mid-December 1953.

## AN IRISH LINK

During Cardiff City's end-of-season Irish tour in May 1925, they spent a few days in Dublin, where they played against Bohemians and were 7-1 winners. Accompanying the group during that part of the tour was Bohemians President, Major-General Emmett Dalton. He had been the right-hand man to Michael Collins, the leader of the IRA during the troubles of 1919 to 1921, when Irish Nationalists fought Britain for home rule. Dalton had been alongside Collins when their convoy was ambushed in County Cork during August 1922 and Collins was killed. During 1919-1921, Dalton had been one of the British Government's most-wanted men, but following the 1922 partition of Ireland into the six Northern counties and the twenty-six counties of the Irish Free State, he was no longer wanted. He maintained cordial relations with Cardiff City for many years after that visit by the club in 1925.

## STAN'S LATE CALL

Locally-born centre-forward Stan Richards, whose middle name was Verdun after the famous First World War battle, played on just one occasion for Wales – against England in a 3-0 defeat during November 1946 at Manchester City's Maine Road ground. He was not an original selection for the match, and found out about his call-up whilst watching a film at a Cardiff cinema. A notice was flashed up on the screen requesting him to attend the cinema manager's office, and he was told by telephone to travel to Manchester immediately. Stan, who joined City at the age of 28 in January 1946 after playing in Services football, then for Cardiff Corries and London club Tufnell Park, scored 30 League goals in the 1946/47 promotion season – a Bluebirds record until it was beaten by Robert Earnshaw in 2002/03. Stan was never particularly keen on training, and his knees often gave him trouble. But if he was ever unwilling to go out training with his colleagues on any particular morning, manager Billy McCandless would often call Stan into his office. A bottle of whisky would be opened, and after a chat and a nip or two, Stan would go out and train! In the summer of 1948, Stan joined Swansea Town, also helping them to promotion, and he ended his career at Barry Town. He died in Cardiff at the age of 70 in 1987.

## MALLOY'S OWN-GOALS

Bluebirds defender Danny Malloy (1955-61) was credited with no fewer than fourteen own-goals during his time with Cardiff City. Most of them were deflections by the former Dundee player, who always threw himself into the thick of the action, never more so than when City played Liverpool in the opening Second Division match of 1959/60 at Ninian Park. After the Bluebirds had taken the lead, Danny twice deflected shots past his own keeper Graham Vearncombe before half-time. City went on to win the game 3-2, and therefore scored all five goals! When City went to Anfield for the return game in mid-December 1959, they won 4-0 in what was Bill Shankly's first match as manager of the Merseyside club.

## THE HALT

Ninian Park was opened in 1910 and adjoined the Taff Vale Railway, whose officials watched the club's early progress with interest. With a keen business sense, they built a small station in November 1912 at the junction of Sloper Road and Leckwith Road, just a couple of hundred yards from the ground. It was known for many years as Ninian Park Halt, but with the privatisation of the railway system over the last twenty years, it is now part of Valley Lines and known simply as Ninian Park.

## POOR START

There is nothing like a good start to a new season, and City's results at the opening of 1913/14 were nothing like a good start to a new season! Newly promoted to Southern League Division One, the Bluebirds lost their first five games, but recovered to finish in mid-table.

## ENGLAND'S RETURN TO NINIAN PARK

Football journalist Harry Ditton, who was 'Citizen' of *The Western Mail* from 1925 to 1935, was instrumental in persuading the FA of Wales that they should reinstate the Wales v England Home International Championship fixtures to Ninian Park after an 11-year gap. Following the game in Cardiff in March 1923, when the fixture attracted a moderate 20,000 crowd, the FAW staged the bi-annual home game against England at Swansea and at Wrexham on the basis that smaller attendances at those grounds would be prepared to pay higher admission charges. But Harry Ditton felt that Cardiff was the centre of Welsh international football and told the FAW Secretary Ted Robbins that if he and his Council agreed to bring England back to Cardiff, then *The Western Mail* would provide all the publicity that was required. So in September 1934, the game returned to Ninian Park in front of a 36,600 attendance. From then on, until the end of the Home International Championships in 1984, England always played Wales at Ninian Park (except in May 1980 at Wrexham) and the fixture always attracted a capacity attendance.

## NICHOLLS FOUGHT BACK

Bluebirds director Sid Nicholls was on his way home from a Cardiff City board meeting, held at the Grand Hotel in Westgate Street on 4 May 1921, when a gang of half-a-dozen men attacked him at 11pm. But the 53-year-old Nicholls, a well-built former Welsh Rugby international forward, could look after himself, and he fought back. The gang fled empty-handed, with a number of them apparently the worse for wear!

## CAPACITY THREAT

In July 1977, Cardiff City were informed by Cardiff County Council that, under the new Safety of Sports Ground Act, Ninian Park needed a number of structural improvements before the start of the 1977/78 season. The club was told that if the improvements were not carried out in time, then the capacity of the ground would be reduced from 46,000 to 10,000! Chairman Stefan Terlezski sought the help of Prime Minister James Callaghan, in whose Cardiff South constituency Ninian Park stood. He advised the club to negotiate with the County Council, who had a statutory duty to enforce the Act. A compromise was reached, and the capacity was set at 16,000 while the work was carried out. It was completed during the first half of that season and a capacity figure of 46,000 was again allowed.

## ON THE STOMP

Cardiff City, then in the Southern League's First Division, announced in March 1920 that they would apply for election to the Football League's Second Division, there being only two divisions in the League at that time. City would have to canvas support from all the League clubs to back their application, which was to be voted upon at the League's Annual General Meeting on 31 May 1920. Midlands League club Leeds United, formed in October 1919 following the disbandment of Leeds City, also applied as did Portsmouth, who went on to win the Southern League Championship while Cardiff City finished fourth. It was the Bluebirds and Leeds who won the votes for the two vacancies in Division Two.

## BLUEBIRDS WHO BECAME LEAGUE MANAGERS

The following Cardiff City players went on to manage League clubs at the end of their playing careers... Gary Bennett, Bill Corkhill, John Cornforth, Stan Davies, Alan Durban, Bobby Ferguson, Brian Fynn, Billy Hardy, Brian Harris, Charlie Jones, Leslie Jones, John Lewis, Jack Mansell, John McSeveney, Ronnie Moore, Richie Morgan, Jimmy Mullen, Russell Osman, Fred Pagnam, David Penney, Kevin Ratcliffe, Fred Stansfield, Phil Stant, Mel Sutton, and John Toshack.

## ARMED PROTECTION

When Cardiff City played at Irish club Derry City in the European Cup Winners' Cup first round first leg during September 1988, it was at a time of continuing civil and political unrest in Northern Ireland. The Bluebirds were accompanied during their stay in the province by an armed RUC plain-clothes officer. They experienced no problems and were given a great welcome, and the RUC officer told the club that it was the best spell of duty that he had ever spent.

## WELSH CUP ATTENDANCE RECORD

When Cardiff City met Swansea Town (as they were then known) in the Welsh Senior Cup Final at Ninian Park on 30 April 1956, the match attracted an attendance of 37,500, which remains an all-time record for the competition. The Bluebirds won that final 3-2, their first success in the Welsh Cup since 1930.

## NO SUB SELECTED

Les Lea, signed by City from Blackpool 24 hours earlier, was due to make his Bluebirds debut against Plymouth at Home Park on 16 December 1967, but a delay over the registration of his transfer with the Football League led to a telephone call from City secretary Graham Keenor to manager Jimmy Scoular warning him not to play Lea. City only had twelve players with them, so intended substitute Gary Bell was included in the eleven, and City played with no substitute on the bench. The sides drew 0-0.

## HOLLYMAN'S LESSONS FROM MATTHEWS

Locally-born wing-half Ken Hollyman joined the club from local football in 1942. After war service in the Royal Navy, he was an outstanding member of City's 1946/47 Third Division (South) Championship side. At the start of the 1949/50 season, it was decided to try him on the right wing. Before the season began, however, he was sent to Blackpool for a week to be tutored by the legendary Stanley Matthews, following a request by City's chairman Herbert Merrett, who wanted Hollyman to be taught what Merrett described as: "the finer arts of wing play". England international Matthews, in a letter of reply to Merrett's request, suggested that his club Blackpool not be informed of this arrangement as City were paying Matthews a fee of ten guineas for his work.

## THE LEVEL CROSSING

Cardiff City supporters visiting Ninian Park will be familiar with the two railway bridges in Leckwith Road. But until 1932, there was one railway bridge, and a level crossing, over which passed the main London-Swansea line. When the crossing gates were closed for the approach of trains, it often caused delays for the football crowds, especially with the large attendances of the 1920s. The Great Western Railway had put a footbridge over the line, but its capacity was limited to a few at a time. In 1932, however, the GWR lowered a section of Leckwith Road and heightened the railway line to include a bridge. Ironically, by that time City's attendances were so low that there were few delays.

## TWENTY-YEAR WAIT

In the early 1980s work began on converting the rear section of the Canton (now Family Spar) Stand into executive boxes and hospitality areas. But a shortage of finance halted the scheme, and the stand remained in an unsightly condition for a number of years. The work was eventually completed in 2001, with the refurbished stand containing viewing areas, hospitality areas and various administrative offices.

## ARSENAL BOSS WANTED TO FIGHT

When Cardiff City defeated Arsenal 1-0 at Ninian Park in Division One on 24 September 1960, the Bluebirds goal was scored by their former Arsenal forward Derek Tapscott, who appeared to put the ball in with his hand. The only person amongst the match officials and the 32,705 crowd who did not see what happened was the referee – and he gave a goal. When Tappy went into the Arsenal dressing-room after the game to meet his former team-mates, there was almost a stand-up fight when Arsenal manager George Swindin came in. Swindin had transferred Tapscott to Cardiff two years previously, as he had no further use for him following Tappy's cartilage operation in August 1957. On seeing Tapscott in his team's dressing-room, and in view of the controversial goal, Swindin lost his temper. He tore off his jacket and wanted to fight Tappy, who was quite prepared to respond. Two Arsenal players bundled their former team-mate out while the rest held Swindin back, and fisticuffs were averted. Two years later, with Tappy still scoring regularly for the Bluebirds, City appointed a new manager – George Swindin!

## DISASTROUS MANAGERIAL SPELL

Welsh international Alan Durban was a successful player with Cardiff City, and moved to Derby County in the summer of 1963, eventually becoming a major part of Brian Clough's team. But when he returned to Cardiff as manager in late September 1984 after spells in charge at Shrewsbury, Stoke and Sunderland, he had a disastrous time. The Bluebirds were relegated at the end of 1984/85 to the old Division Three, and in 1985/86 went down again to Division Four.

## FERGUSON'S TRAGIC END

FA Cup-winning hero Hughie Ferguson, who had scored the only goal in the Bluebirds' 1927 win over Arsenal, was found dead next to a gas-ring in the Dundee trainers' room on 8 January 1930, having taken his own life. Ferguson had left Cardiff City for Dundee in the summer of 1929, but had been unable to reproduce his goal-scoring success and had become depressed. He was 33, and left a wife and two young sons.

# FIRST EVER-PRESENT

The first Cardiff City player to have a 100% appearance record for the club in a season's League matches was Scottish-born right-back Jimmy Nelson, who had been signed from Belfast Crusaders in the summer of 1921. Nelson played in all 42 First Division games for City in 1923/24, when they narrowly failed, on goal average, to win the League Championship. City also played six FA Cup matches and six Welsh Cup matches that season, Nelson appearing in eleven of them – so he missed just one of the Bluebirds' 58 first-team matches that season.

# FARQUHARSON'S MATTER OF PRINCIPLE

Cardiff City's Irish international goalkeeper Tom Farquharson refused to accept his selection for the Home International Championship fixture against Scotland at Ibrox Park on 19 September 1931 because of what he described as a 'matter of principle'. Farquharson objected to the Irish Football Association (representing the six counties of Northern Ireland after the 1922 partition of the country) picking an all-Ireland side when the 26 counties of the Irish Free State came under the Free State FA that had been officially recognised by FIFA in 1923. Farquharson stated he would have taken the same position if the Free State FA had selected an all-Ireland team to include players from the six Northern Counties. Prior to his refusal, Farquharson had played for all-Ireland teams, but now felt that it was time to highlight the situation. Despite Farquharson's position, the Irish Football Association continued to select players born from throughout Ireland until 1949, when the Free State declared itself a republic. From then on, the Free State FA selected its own international teams, but by that time Farquharson had been retired for fourteen years. City's keeper had made no secret of the fact that when he left Ireland in 1920 to come to South Wales looking for work during the troubles (1919-21), he was a committed nationalist who wanted home rule for Ireland. Farquharson carried a hand-gun in his kit-bag during his years with Cardiff City (1922-35), and told team-mates that he did so because of "certain persons" in Ireland.

## RUGBY WRITER'S VIEW

*Western Mail* Sports Editor J B G Thomas was one of the world's leading Rugby Union journalists and authors. Football was not really his sport, but in late September 1970 he was on holiday in Cyprus when Cardiff City played the second leg of their European Cup Winners Cup first round match against PO Larnaca. As City had won the home leg 8-0, Thomas decided that it was not worth sending the newspaper's football correspondent to report on the game and covered it himself. He did not have much about which to write – it was a 0-0 draw.

## A SAD DECLINE

When Cardiff City suffered their second relegation in two years at the end of 1930/31, falling into the Third Division (South), the Ninian Park attendance for the final game of that season against Bury on 2 May 1931 was 3841. Ten years earlier, on 27 August 1921, the opening match in Division One against FA Cup holders Tottenham Hotspur at Ninian Park saw the official attendance recorded as 51,000 – plus an estimated 7000-8000 who broke through the gates after the turnstiles were closed before the kick-off.

## CURTIS WALKED OUT

Cardiff-born Ernie Curtis, the youngest member of the Bluebirds' 1927 FA Cup-winning team, returned to Cardiff City from Birmingham City in November 1933 after moving from Ninian Park in March 1928. But after a disagreement over wages at the end of 1933/34, he refused to re-sign for the Bluebirds, and became landlord of a public house in Birmingham, with his registration still being retained by Cardiff City. He was officially transferred to Coventry City in February 1935. He later became their player-coach, and during the Second World War joined the Royal Artillery. He was captured in the Far East by the Japanese and was a prisoner of war from 1942 to 1945. Curtis eventually returned to Ninian Park in July 1956 to join the club's training staff, remaining until 1965, and died at the age of 85 in 1992.

## NAMING NAMES

Charlie Oatway was signed by Cardiff City from non-league West London club Yeading in August 1994. His full name took up quite some space on his contract as, when he was born, his parents gave him the first names of the entire Queens Park Rangers promotion side of 1972/73. His full names are Anthony Philip David Terry Frank Donald Stanley Gerry Gordon Stephen James Oatway – but everyone knew him as 'Charlie'.

## SELECTED AS GOALKEEPER

Bluebirds full-back Arthur Layton tried out as a goalkeeper in a Welsh League home match against Aberaman during the 1919/20 season. The former Aston Villa and Middlesbrough player had done well enough in training to be given an opportunity, and on 20 March 1920 played in goal for the first team at Brighton in the Southern League in a 1-1 draw, and again four days later against Swansea Town in the Welsh Cup semi-final at Ninian Park, when City were 2-1 winners.

## VINCENT'S DEBUT BLUEBIRDS GOAL

Midfield player Johnny Vincent was signed from Middlesbrough for £35,000 on 12 October 1972. Two days later, he made his City debut at Ninian Park, and scored in a 2-0 victory – against Middlesbrough!

## AN EARLY CHRISTMAS PRESENT FOR THE LADIES

The Bluebirds announced in their match programme for the friendly game against Plymouth Argyle on 20 December 1919 that they had built a ladies' 'retiring room' at Ninian Park next to the secretary's office. This was presumably a polite way of saying that it was a female washroom and toilet. It was also announced in the same programme that the club had installed a much-needed convenience for gentlemen in the Grandstand enclosure, and that they intended to build others in various parts of the ground. How everyone had managed up to then is anyone's guess!

## LOCKING AWAY THE WHISKY!

The directors, at their weekly meeting on 5 October 1938, discussed the question of the boardroom whisky. It appeared that their match day guests had been taking more than their fair share before the game and at half-time, getting to their seats after the start of each half following a few extra nips! After a lengthy discussion on the matter, the board decided to install a box in a cupboard, and to lock the bottles away during the game.

## CAP-IN-HAND

Before relegation and promotion between the Football League and the Conference League, clubs that finished in the bottom two places of the two regionalised lowest divisions had to resign from the Football League and seek re-election by their fellow clubs. At the end of 1933/34, Cardiff City finished bottom of Division Three (South), just seven years after winning the FA Cup as an established First Division side, and had to go cap-in-hand to the Annual General Meeting of the Football League on 4 June 1934 to apply for re-election. There was no question of City being kicked out, and they were comfortably voted back in.

## FIVE OR MORE

Seven players have scored five or more goals in League or Cup games for Cardiff City. On 1 September 1928, Hugh Ferguson hit five in the 7-0 First Division home win over Burnley. Walter Robbins scored five in the 6-0 Third Division (South) 9-2 home win over Thames on 6 February 1932, while on 2 April 1933, Jim Henderson netted five times in the 6-0 Third Division (South) home win over Northampton Town. On 17 March 1956, Gerry Hitchens obtained five in the Welsh Cup semi-final 7-0 win against Oswestry at Wrexham. Derek Tapscott scored six in the 16-0 Welsh Cup home win over Knighton Town on 28 January 1961. On 21 January 1970, Brian Clark scored five against Barmouth at Ninian Park in the Welsh Cup, and finally, Gavin Gordon hit five in the 7-1 home win over Rushden and Diamonds in the LDV Vans Trophy on 16 October 2001.

## NINIAN ROCKERS

Bob Marley performed at Ninian Park on 19 June 1976 in his West Coast Rock Show that was part of his Rastaman Vibration Tour. The line-up on the night also included Country Joe McDonald and the Fish, the Eric Burden Band, the Sutherland Brothers and Quiver, the Pretty Things, Gloria Jones, and Gonzalez.

## WEDDING-DAY GOAL

On Saturday 28 December 1957, Cardiff City winger Colin Hudson was married at a Newport church. After a brief stay at his wedding reception, Hudson and his best man Alan Harrington rushed by car to Ninian Park where they both played for City in their Second Division match against Liverpool, Hudson scoring City's opening goal in their 6-1 victory.

## CHRISTMAS PARCELS FOR THE BOYS

Cardiff City took a collection during the friendly match against Barnsley at Ninian Park on 27 December 1915 to raise money so that parcels of comforts could be sent to players Fred Keenor and Jack Stephenson, who were in action with the British Army in France. Both sent letters of thanks, in which they expressed the view that the war would end in 1916. They were wrong – it lasted until November 1918.

## TRAINER HAD TO PLAY

On 2 January 1922, Cardiff City were on their way to Blackburn Rovers after an overnight stay at Southport when two of their players – inside-forward Jimmy Gill and left-winger Jack Evans – were found to be suffering from influenza. As the Bluebirds had travelled north with just twelve players (the selected eleven and a travelling reserve), they were left with ten men. Trainer George Latham was signed on emergency forms and a telegram was sent to the Football League. Latham duly played in City's 3-1 win, and at forty-two years of age was Cardiff City's oldest-ever debut-maker.

## A PORTSMOUTH BLUEBIRDS STREET

A newly-built street of terraced houses in Portsmouth, completed in 1921, was named Ninian Park Road. The builder and developer was a local Councillor named Richard Brittan. His son Charlie was captain of Cardiff City, who had just won promotion to Division One and reached the semi-final of the FA Cup in what was their debut season in League football. Brittan senior therefore named the street after the ground where his son regularly played.

## IT'S NEVER ALL OVER

The 1951/52 season ended in Cardiff City's promotion back to top level (the original Division One) for the first time since 1929. But with a few games left, it looked all over for the Bluebirds. Only the top two went up in those days, and Sheffield Wednesday were a few points clear in top place, going on to win the title. Birmingham were in second spot with a far better goal average than Cardiff City. Even if City, at that stage, won their final four games and Birmingham won their remaining three, the Midlands side would still finish second. But on 19 April 1952, when City were at Luton and Birmingham were at Notts County, the whole situation changed dramatically! City kicked off at 3.15pm, fifteen minutes later than Birmingham. At half-time Birmingham were 3-0 down, while City trailed 2-1 in their match at Kenilworth Road. Manager Cyril Spiers came to the touchline to tell his players that they had to avoid defeat, and they did so with a 2-2 draw. Birmingham lost 5-0 and now had a worse goal average than City, who had three games left against Birmingham's two. The Midlands team were two points ahead (two for a win in those days), and it meant that even if Birmingham won those last two, City could win their remaining three (all at Ninian Park) and go up on goal-average. That is exactly what happened – Birmingham finished with two wins to reach fifty-one points and went off on tour to Holland. City beat Blackburn 3-1 in front of 36,000 two days after drawing at Luton. They then beat Bury 3-0 before 40,000. And on FA Cup Final day 1952, in their game in hand, they beat Leeds United 3-1 in front of a joyous 51,000 crowd – it's never all over…

## SHANKLY THE ONE-MATCH BLUEBIRD

Legendary Liverpool manager Bill Shankly played once for Cardiff City. During the 1939-45 War, players in the Forces could turn out as guests in wartime regional football for the club nearest to where they were based. During 1942, Shankly, then a Preston North End and Scotland wing-half, was stationed at RAF St Athan. On 3 October 1942, City manager Cyril Spiers invited him to play at Ninian Park against Lovells Athletic, the Newport-based confectionery manufacturers team, in a League West match. His match-fee was thirty shillings (£1.50), but in conversation with the Lovells players whose firm was producing wartime rations for the Forces, Shankly discovered that they received £5 per match. So he never played for City again, and joined Lovells!

## BLUEBIRDS RAN UP SIXTEEN!

Following Cardiff City's £350 fine by the FA of Wales for fielding a reserve side in their Welsh Cup win at Swansea Town in March 1960, the Bluebirds responded by playing their full first-team against mid-Wales League side Knighton Town in a Welsh Cup fifth round tie at Ninian Park the following season on 28 January 1961. City, then midway in Division One, were 16-0 winners and goalkeeper Maurice Swan touched the ball on just one occasion, when a team-mate remembered him with a back-pass. Two players managed hat-tricks: Derek Tapscott netted six times, while Graham Moore scored four. Defender and skipper Danny Malloy played the second half in attack, and also put his name on the scoresheet in an easy win for City.

## FORMER TENNIS PRO

Loan signing Michael Boulding, who came to Cardiff City from Barnsley in March 2005, was a professional tennis player before taking up football full-time. Boulding competed in tournaments around the world, and often roomed with Tim Henman on the various tennis circuits. But after several years of competition, he decided to concentrate on a football career.

## GAMMON AND LAW

Swansea-born Steve Gammon was an outstanding wing-half (midfield player) with Cardiff City whom he joined as a junior in 1957 from Mumbles Boys' Club. He represented Wales at under-23 level, and played in City's promotion-winning squad of 1959/60 when the club reached the old Division One. But after becoming a regular in 1960/61, with a great future ahead of him, he broke his leg as a result of a controversial tackle by Manchester City's Denis Law at Ninian Park on 4 February 1961. Gammon did return to action the following December, but was never able to reach his previous standard, and in fact broke the same leg on two further occasions. In 1965, he moved to Kettering Town where he was later manager. After his playing career ended, he ran a highly successful garden equipment firm in Northamptonshire, where he still lives.

## NO PLAY-OFF GOALS CONCEDED

Cardiff City became the first club to go through the current play-off system of three matches without conceding a goal. In the 2003 semi-final, they defeated Bristol City 1-0 at Ninian Park and drew 0-0 at Ashton Gate. In the Final, they defeated Queens Park Rangers 1-0.

## BIG H

Grangetown-born Harry Parsons worked for the club from 1966 until his retirement in 1996 at the age of 78. A wartime soldier with Field Marshal Montgomery's Eighth Army in North Africa, Italy and Europe, Harry was a delivery driver with Braddons, a Cardiff fruit and vegetable wholesalers based at Bessemer Road Market. He had been involved with local football for many years, and in his first three seasons with the club he was a part-time local scout for manager Jimmy Scoular, and also looked after the youth-team. Harry became a full-time employee in 1969, acting as youth-team manager, assistant trainer, kit manager and general factotum behind the scenes on the playing side. 'Big H', as he was popularly known by everyone, was well known to generations of Cardiff City players. He died in February 2006 at the age of 87.

## THE LAST-SECOND CORNER-KICK WINNER

A change in the rules by FIFA in the summer of 1924 allowed a goal to be scored direct from a corner-kick. The first player to do so in League or Cup was Huddersfield's Billy Smith, in his team's 4-0 First Division home win over Arsenal in October 1924. The second "corner-kick goal" was much more crucial. It came in the FA Cup quarter-final between Cardiff City and Leicester at Ninian Park on 7 March 1925. With the very last kick of the match, and the teams level at 1-1, City's Welsh international winger Billy Davies took a flag-kick from the Bob Bank/Grange End corner. He swerved the ball in with his right foot, and it crossed the goal-line before Leicester keeper Bert Godderidge got a hand to it. Referee Ernest Pinkston of Birmingham immediately blew for time, but many of the 50,272 spectators did not realise that the Bluebirds had won until Davies and skipper Jimmy Blair confirmed the result from the stand to thousands of fans waiting on the pitch! City went on to lose 1-0 in the final against Sheffield United.

## BIG MONEY

In November 1925, Cardiff City, near the wrong end of Division One, spent £8,000 – a huge sum at the time – on Clyde winger George McLachlan (£3000) and Motherwell centre-forward Hughie Ferguson, who cost a club record £5000. A prolific scorer in Scottish football, Ferguson netted on his City debut in a 5-2 home win over Leicester City. He scored 19 League goals in 26 appearances that season, helping City to avoid relegation. He went on to play against Arsenal in the FA Cup Final the following season, and was credited with the goal in City's 1-0 victory.

## WARBOYS' FOURSOME

Former Sheffield Wednesday forward Alan Warboys scored Cardiff City's quickest ever hat-trick against Carlisle United on 6 March 1971. He netted after two, five, and ten minutes – and he completed the scoring two minutes before half-time with his fourth goal of the game. The win took City to the top of Division Two.

## SPIERS' CONTRACTUAL DISAGREEMENT

Manager Cyril Spiers, who had joined the club in April 1939, resigned to take charge at Norwich City in the summer of 1946. Spiers, a former goalkeeper with Aston Villa, Tottenham and Wolves, where he had also been assistant manager, had managed the Bluebirds throughout the war on a reduced salary, on the understanding that when peacetime returned, he would be reimbursed. But when the time came, the directors told him that the club's financial position meant that they were not able to do so, and they suggested instead an improved promotion bonus. So Spiers gave notice that he would seek another managerial job, and he joined Norwich in June 1946. He was replaced by former Newport County manager Billy McCandless, and so well did City recover financially in the 1946/47 period that when McCandless left for Swansea Town in November 1947, Spiers was happy to return to Ninian Park on improved terms, and he remained until May 1954.

## LEFT IN COWBRIDGE!

Bluebirds centre-forward Fred Pagnam and defender Bert Smith were well-known practical jokers in City's dressing-room. They had played a trick on skipper Charlie Brittan, who wanted to get his own back. In April 1921, a few days before the final match of the season, with promotion to Division One having been secured, Brittan, a local City Councillor, invited Pagnam and Smith on a taxi-ride to Cowbridge where he said he had some business. On their arrival, they called at the Bear Hotel for a drink, Brittan having asked the taxi to wait. He told Pagnam and Smith that he would be absent for half an hour whilst attending to his business. He then took the taxi back to Cardiff, telling the driver that the other two had decided to stay. After an hour or so, Pagnam and Smith became a little concerned at Brittan's absence. They went outside to look, but there was no sign of him or the taxi. In those early days of country motoring, there was little or no traffic passing through Cowbridge at that time of the evening. Pagnam and Smith had no choice but to walk the ten miles back to Cardiff along the A48, and it took them nearly three hours to get home. In the dressing-room the next morning at training, the other players were highly amused at this turn of events – Pagnam and Smith never troubled Brittan again!

## CARDIFF CITY CHAIRMEN

| Name | From | To |
| --- | --- | --- |
| Sid Nicholls | July 1910 | August 1914 |
| J A McFarlane | August 1914 | August 1919 |
| Dr Alex Brownlee | August 1919 | September 1920 |
| Walter Riden | September 1920 | June 1921 |
| John Pritchard | June 1921 | November 1921 |
| Walter Empsall | November 1921 | August 1923 |
| Charles Cox | August 1923 | August 1924 |
| Dr William Nicholson | August 1924 | August 1925 |
| Sid Nicholls | August 1925 | August 1926 |
| Walter Parker | August 1926 | August 1927 |
| Watkin J Williams* | August 1927 | December 1927 |
| Walter Parker | December 1927 | August 1929 |
| Dr Alex Brownlee | August 1929 | August 1930 |
| Walter Riden | August 1930 | August 1932 |
| Dr William Nicholson | August 1932 | August 1933 |
| Walter Parker | August 1933 | August 1934 |
| Dr Alex Brownlee | August 1934 | November 1934 |
| Tudor Steer | November 1934 | December 1934 |
| Dr Alex Brownlee | December 1934 | August 1935 |
| Tudor Steer | August 1935 | September 1936 |
| Dr James Wade | September 1936 | August 1937 |
| Chris Page | August 1937 | September 1938 |
| William Forbes | October 1938 | April 1939 |
| Herbert Merrett | April 1939 | February 1953 |
| John Morgan | February 1953 | May 1954 |
| Sir Herbert Merrett | May 1954 | June 1957 |
| Ron Beecher+ | June 1957 | January 1964 |
| Fred Dewey | January 1964 | October 1972 |
| David Goldstone | October 1972 | July 1975 |
| Stefan Terlezski | July 1975 | October 1977 |
| Bob Grogan | November 1977 | August 1983 |
| Jack Leonard | August 1983 | May 1986 |
| Tony Clemo | June 1986 | June 1992 |
| Rick Wright | June 1992 | July 1995 |
| Samesh Kumar | July 1995 | May 1999 |

Steve Borley......................May 1999..........................August 2000
Sam Hammam ................August 2000......................January 2007
Peter Ridsdale..................January 2007

*\* Watkin J. Williams resigned in December 1927 after being convicted*
*of administration offences in connection with his shipping line.*
*+ Ron Beecher died in January 1964*

## ROYAL SPECTATORS

When Cardiff played Wolves at Liverpool's Anfield in the FA Cup semi-final on 19 March 1921, King George V and Queen Mary arrived just before half-time after watching the Grand National at Aintree. Both teams were presented to the King before the start of the second half, and it remains the only occasion when Royalty has attended an FA Cup semi-final. The teams drew 0-0.

## QUICK-FIRE ROBBINS

The best-ever scoring sequence by a Cardiff City player was achieved by Welsh international winger Walter Robbins in February 1932, when he netted eleven times in four consecutive League and Cup matches. On 6 February he scored five times in City's 9-2 home win over East London club Thames in Division Three (South). He netted three in the Bluebirds' Welsh Cup fifth round 5-3 win at Llanelli two days later, then one more in City's 3-2 League win at Brentford on 13 February. Finally, he scored twice in City's 5-2 League win against Exeter City at Ninian Park on 20 February.

## LAST CHRISTMAS DAY MATCH AT NINIAN PARK

A regular feature of holiday League fixtures for many years was the Christmas Day match. These were usually 11am kick-offs, and continued until the late 1950s, when the Football League decided to end matches on that day. The last Christmas Day match at Ninian Park was in 1954, against West Bromwich Albion in Division One, when the Bluebirds were 3-2 winners in front of a 22,845 attendance.

## WORLD WAR ONE HEROES

During the 1915/16 season, Fred Keenor, in training with the British Army in France, was able to play for the 17th Middlesex Regiment in the Divisional Cup, which his team won. He took part in the Battle of the Somme in July 1916, and sustained wounds that resulted in him being repatriated back to a hospital in Dublin, then part of the United Kingdom. Jack Stephenson was badly wounded in action, and never played again. Of the many Cardiff City players who joined the Forces in World War One, Tom Witts and Ken McKenzie were killed in action, while former City winger Billy Stewart, who had played in the Bluebirds' opening season of 1910/11, was killed in action at the Dardanelles in 1915. Trainer George Latham, who had fought in the ranks in the Boer War (1899-1902), reached the rank of Captain, and was awarded the Military Cross for bravery in action in the Middle East in 1917 during the first Battle of Gaza against Turkish forces.

## HOME GOAL AVALANCHE

City's three home games during December 1957 saw them score eighteen goals! They defeated Barnsley 7-0 on 7 December, Stoke City 5-2 on Boxing Day, and Liverpool 6-1 on 28 December. Their attendances during that spell were 8941 (Barnsley), 23,638 (Stoke), and 30,622 (Liverpool).

## PENALTY FAILURE COSTS CITY THE TITLE

Cardiff City went into their final First Division game of the season at Birmingham on 3 May 1924 leading the League Championship by one point from Huddersfield Town, whose final game was at home to Nottingham Forest. City were on 56 points, Huddersfield were on 55, and in those days there were two points for a win. Victory would ensure that City won the title. *The Western Mail*, in its preview of the situation on the Saturday morning, looked at a number of possibilities, one of which was as follows: 'City fans can find consolation in the knowledge that, should their side only draw 0-0, Huddersfield who are not prolific scorers, would have to win 3-0.' In the end, that is precisely what happened – and the Bluebirds missed a second-half penalty, Len Davies seeing his spot-kick saved by Birmingham's goalkeeper Dan Tremelling.

## FOOTBALL LEAGUE DIVISION ONE

|  | Pl | W | D | L | F | A | W | D | L | F | A | Pts |
|---|---|---|---|---|---|---|---|---|---|---|---|---|
| Huddersfield Town | 42 | 15 | 5 | 1 | 35 | 9 | 8 | 6 | 7 | 25 | 24 | 57 |
| CARDIFF CITY | 42 | 14 | 5 | 2 | 35 | 13 | 8 | 8 | 5 | 26 | 21 | 57 |
| Sunderland | 42 | 12 | 7 | 2 | 38 | 20 | 10 | 2 | 9 | 33 | 34 | 53 |
| Bolton Wanderers | 42 | 13 | 6 | 2 | 45 | 13 | 5 | 8 | 8 | 23 | 21 | 50 |
| Sheff United | 42 | 12 | 5 | 4 | 39 | 16 | 7 | 7 | 7 | 30 | 33 | 50 |
| Aston Villa | 42 | 10 | 10 | 1 | 33 | 11 | 8 | 3 | 10 | 19 | 26 | 49 |
| Everton | 42 | 13 | 7 | 1 | 43 | 18 | 5 | 6 | 10 | 19 | 35 | 49 |
| Blackburn Rovers | 42 | 14 | 5 | 2 | 40 | 13 | 3 | 6 | 12 | 14 | 37 | 45 |
| Newcastle United | 42 | 13 | 5 | 3 | 40 | 21 | 4 | 5 | 12 | 20 | 33 | 44 |
| Notts County | 42 | 9 | 7 | 5 | 21 | 15 | 5 | 7 | 9 | 23 | 34 | 42 |
| Man City | 42 | 11 | 7 | 3 | 34 | 24 | 4 | 5 | 12 | 20 | 47 | 42 |
| Liverpool | 42 | 11 | 5 | 5 | 35 | 20 | 4 | 6 | 11 | 14 | 28 | 41 |
| West Ham | 42 | 10 | 6 | 5 | 26 | 17 | 3 | 9 | 9 | 14 | 26 | 41 |
| Birmingham | 42 | 10 | 4 | 7 | 25 | 19 | 3 | 9 | 9 | 16 | 30 | 39 |
| Tottenham | 42 | 9 | 6 | 6 | 30 | 22 | 3 | 8 | 10 | 20 | 34 | 38 |
| West Brom | 42 | 10 | 6 | 5 | 43 | 30 | 2 | 8 | 11 | 8 | 32 | 38 |
| Burnley | 42 | 10 | 5 | 6 | 39 | 27 | 2 | 7 | 12 | 16 | 33 | 36 |
| Preston | 42 | 8 | 4 | 9 | 34 | 27 | 4 | 6 | 11 | 18 | 40 | 34 |
| Arsenal | 42 | 8 | 5 | 8 | 25 | 24 | 4 | 4 | 13 | 15 | 39 | 33 |
| Nottm Forest | 42 | 7 | 9 | 5 | 19 | 15 | 3 | 3 | 15 | 23 | 49 | 32 |
| Chelsea | 42 | 7 | 9 | 5 | 23 | 21 | 2 | 5 | 14 | 8 | 32 | 32 |
| Middlesbro | 42 | 6 | 4 | 11 | 23 | 23 | 1 | 4 | 16 | 14 | 37 | 22 |

At the time, the method of deciding positions when clubs were level on points was by goal average (goals-for divided by goals-against). When the 1923/24 positions were worked out, Huddersfield took the title with a fractionally better goal average than City, the difference between them being 0.024 of a goal! If modern rules had applied, the two sides would have been level on goal difference, but City would have won the title by virtue of having scored one more goal than Huddersfield.

# OUTSTANDING FULL-BACK

Aberaman-born Alf Sherwood was the greatest full-back to have played for Cardiff City. He joined the club in 1941/42 as an 18-year old, having been with his local side Aberaman Athletic. A Wales schoolboy international at both football and cricket, he was then working in the coal-mines as a 'Bevin Boy' under a scheme devised by Ernest Bevin, then Minister of Power, in which teenage boys from all classes of society were selected by ballot to work as miners instead of joining the Armed Forces. Sherwood was a half-back when he joined City, but was switched to full-back by manager Cyril Spiers. He remained a part-timer with City until peacetime football resumed in 1946. At his peak, Sherwood was regarded as the finest full-back in Europe, and as such was awarded the Graydon Medal in 1949. He first represented Wales in a 'Victory' International against Ireland in 1946, and went on to make 39 peacetime appearances for his country whilst with City. In the summer of 1956, at the age of 33, Sherwood was transferred to Newport County, with whom he played for five seasons, gaining a further two Welsh caps in 1956/57. He was also a more-than-useful emergency goalkeeper, standing in for City on several occasions for injured keepers during matches before the use of substitutes. In hindsight, it was a mistake for City to have let him go, his steady influence being missed when The Bluebirds went down from Division One in 1956/57. It was often said that Sherwood, who was exceptionally quick in the tackle and in his recovery when beaten, was one of only two full-backs who could effectively hold the legendary Blackpool and England winger Stan (late Sir Stanley) Matthews. The other one was Birmingham City's Welsh international Billy Hughes. City supporters held the view that Matthews would never play against Sherwood at Ninian Park, though they did face each other in a number of international and club matches. Only on two occasions did they oppose each other in Cardiff – in the 1955/56 season, when Wales beat England 2-1 in October 1955 and City beat Blackpool 1-0 in February 1956. After leaving Newport, Sherwood was player/manager at Southern League Barry Town, and was later a security officer with the National Coal Board. He died at the age of 66 in March 1990, after suffering a major heart-attack whilst playing golf.

## UNDEFEATED HOME RUNS

The 24,572 fans who saw Cardiff City play Leyton Orient at Ninian Park in Division Three (South) on 7 June 1947, in what was the final game of that season, were expecting nothing less than victory. It was City's 21st home League game of 1946/47, and they were unbeaten at Ninian Park. The Bluebirds won 1-0, and in winning the divisional title were unbeaten at home in a season for the first time since entering League football in 1920. The only other occasion on which City have gone through a season unbeaten at home was in 2000/01, when they won promotion as runners-up in Division Three.

## DO YOU KNOW THE PIANO IS ON MY FOOT?

In December 1965, Cardiff City's locally-born apprentice John Toshack went with several of his colleagues to collect a piano from the Dorset Street home in Grangetown of City fan Alan Giles. The piano was to be taken to the Bluebirds Club behind the Canton Stand at Ninian Park, where Mr Giles was in a group that played for the members on dance nights. Unfortunately, the apprentices could not hold the piano as they lifted it into the club's van, and it fell onto Toshack's foot, breaking a bone! He was out of action for several weeks, much to the displeasure of manager Jimmy Scoular. That incident has never been forgotten by Mr Giles's eldest son David – he saw the whole affair as a ten-year-old boy when he returned home from school that afternoon. David, who was to play for Cardiff City, Wrexham, Swansea City, Newport County and Wales during his career, was often reminded of that incident by the TV advert for tea featuring chimpanzees… "Do you know the piano is on my foot?" – "No, you hum it and I'll play it".

## SENGHENYDD CHARITY MATCH

Following the colliery disaster at Senghenydd in October 1913, when over 400 miners were killed, reigning League Champions Blackburn Rovers visited Ninian Park to play Southern League Cardiff City on 17 November in a charity match for the Lord Mayor of Cardiff's Relief Fund. A 15,000 attendance saw City beaten 2-1, but the match raised a considerable amount for the Fund.

## ELEVEN-GOAL THRILLER?

Moscow Dynamo came to Britain in November 1945 on a four-match tour to mark the Anglo-Russian alliance during the Second World War, and they played Cardiff City at Ninian Park on 17 November 1945 in their second match. Dynamo had met Chelsea at Stamford Bridge in their first game, drawing 3-3 in front of an official 74,000 attendance. The true attendance was thought to be in the region of 90,000, many having gained admittance in various non-legitimate ways. Fears of a similar situation kept the Ninian Park crowd to 31,000 (the club had expected over 50,000) and they saw Moscow Dynamo beat Cardiff City's hapless Third Division (South) squad 10-1! When Dynamo, a side sponsored by the KGB, had arrived in Cardiff, they were welcomed by City's chairman Herbert Merrett, who was a major South Wales industrialist. He took them to various places of commercial interest – a situation described in a local paper of a capitalist looking after communists! On the day before the game, the Dynamo players visited a colliery at Abercynon, toured Cardiff Docks, visited the city's civic buildings including the National Museum of Wales, and were given an official welcome by the Lord Mayor of Cardiff, Alderman W. R. Wills.

## GRIMSHAW'S LEAGUE CAP

The first Cardiff City player to appear in a Football League representative team was right-winger Billy Grimshaw, whom City had signed from Bradford City in 1919 when the Bluebirds were in the Southern League. Burnley-born Grimshaw was in the Football League side that beat the Scottish League 3-0 at Ibrox Stadium on 18 March 1922.

## ALWAYS ON TIME

There were never any problems with buses or trams to and from Ninian Park on match days in the mid-to-late 1930s. One of City's directors was William Forbes, who was chairman from October 1938 to April 1939. He was also the General Manager of the Cardiff City Corporation Transport Department, and his employees knew there would be trouble if they did not provide prompt services.

## LUCKY MASCOT

At the end of 1980/81, Cardiff City were in severe danger of relegation from Division Two, but a 0-0 home draw against FA Cup holders West Ham United in the final game on 6 May 1981 saved them on goal difference. The Bluebirds' match-mascot that day was ten-year-old Mario Risoli, son of Italian Cardiff restaurateur Rio Risoli. Mario went on to become a well-known football journalist, and still covers Cardiff City. It was a pity that young Mario was not the match-mascot twelve months later on 17 May 1982, when City needed to beat already-promoted Luton Town to stay in the old Second Division. They lost 3-2, and went down!

## FIRST AND LAST

Londoner Jimmy Gilligan joined Cardiff City in the summer of 1987 from Lincoln City, who had just become the first club to be relegated out of the Football League into the Conference. Gilligan began 1987/88 by scoring Cardiff's first goal of the season in a 1-1 home draw against Leyton Orient, and scored a total of 25 League and Cup goals (19 League, six Cup), including City's last goal of that season in their 2-0 Welsh Cup Final victory over Wrexham at Swansea, which completed a Fourth Division promotion and Welsh Cup double.

## SHERWOOD'S SAVE – LIVERPOOL RELEGATED!

Cardiff City's Welsh international full-back Alf Sherwood was a good basketball player, and it was his handling skills that saw him nominated as the Bluebirds' emergency goalkeeper during matches, if required, before the advent of substitutes. On 17 April 1954, City were playing relegation favourites Liverpool at Anfield in a First Division game. Bluebirds goalkeeper Ronnie Howells fractured his thumb on a goal-post in making a save, so Alf took over for the rest of the match. He made a double save from a penalty taken by Scottish international winger Billy Liddell. City were 1-0 winners, and as a result Liverpool were more or less certain of relegation to Division Two. They didn't return for eight years, but came back under Bill Shankly.

## LONG-TIME ABSENCE

The longest amount of time that Cardiff City have gone since playing any particular club in competitive or other matches (up to 2007) is 47 years. It was in 1959/60 that City last played Liverpool, defeating them 3-2 at Ninian Park and 4-0 at Anfield during that season in the old Division Two. In the years since, the Bluebirds have met every club currently in League or Premiership football in League matches except Accrington Stanley, Dagenham & Redbridge and Morecambe, none of whom City have ever met in the League.

## MARATHON CUP TIE

On 14 April 1945, Cardiff City and Bristol City met at Ninian Park in the second leg of their wartime Football League Cup (North) second round tie. The Bluebirds had won the first leg at Ashton Gate 2-1 the previous week, but the return match at Ninian Park was to last for a remarkable 202 minutes of playing time! The teams were level on goal aggregate at the end of 90 minutes, with Bristol City leading 2-1 on the day. The rules of the competition stated that there should be two ten-minute periods of extra time, and if the teams were then still level, play should continue until a deciding goal was scored. The match had started at 3pm, and including intervals, finished at 6.40pm! Spectators living in the Leckwith, Grangetown and Canton areas went home for tea and, hearing the continuing noise of the crowd, returned to watch the closing stages which ended when Cardiff's Billy Rees scored the deciding goal to make it 2-2, and give the Bluebirds a 3-2 aggregate victory. As for Bristol City, they missed the last train home and had to stay in Cardiff overnight.

## NOT A SELLING CLUB

1910/11 FA Cup winners Bradford City made a £300 offer – a large sum in those days – for the transfer of Cardiff City winger Jack Evans, who a year earlier had been the club's first professional signing. But the Bluebirds' directors declined the offer, and Evans, who became City's first-ever international in 1912, was to remain with the club until April 1926.

## MATCH OF THE DAY DEBUT

Cardiff City's first appearances on BBC Television's *Match of the Day* were in the 1968/69 season. On Saturday 4 January 1969, the FA Cup third round tie against Arsenal at Ninian Park, when 55,136 saw a 0-0 draw, was featured on the programme. On Saturday 8 February 1969, the Second Division match against Oxford United at Ninian Park was a late inclusion. Because of the severe weather throughout the country, only four football League games were played on that day, two of them in Division Two and two in Division Three. Promotion-challenging City beat Oxford 5-0 to go joint second in Division Two, four points behind Derby County. The Bluebirds had been featured on previous occasions on BBC Wales, but these had been for matches in the European Cup Winners' Cup and Welsh Cup.

## COMMENTARY CANDIDATES

The Football Combination reserve-team fixture at Ninian Park between Cardiff City and Swindon Town on 9 October 1954 was used by BBC (Welsh Region) as an audition for several prospective radio commentators. None of the candidates proved suitable.

## WOOLLER SCORED FOR CITY

One of Wales's greatest all-round sportsmen was a registered amateur player with Cardiff City. Wilf Wooller, born in Rhos-on-Sea, North Wales, played Rugby Union for Cambridge University, Sale, London Welsh, the Barbarians, Cardiff and Wales. A Welsh squash international, he played cricket for Denbighshire and Glamorgan (1938-62) and was Glamorgan's secretary from 1947 until 1977. He was also a Test Selector from 1958 to 1961. His Bluebirds involvement began in 1939, when he worked for Cardiff City's chairman Herbert Merrett's coal-exporting firm Guest, Llewellyn and Merrett at Cardiff Docks. Wooller signed as an amateur for City, and played against Fulham in Billy Hardy's Testimonial Match at Ninian Park on 2 May 1939, scoring a goal in City's 3-2 defeat – but his many sporting and business commitments prevented him from playing for the Bluebirds again.

## GREAT START FOR RATCLIFFE

Cardiff City created major headlines in early January 1993 when they signed the former Everton and Wales captain Kevin Ratcliffe, who had just left the Merseyside club after a memorable career, during which he had won a number of honours. Defender Ratcliffe joined City on a match-by-match arrangement, and had a great start with the Bluebirds, heading a late winner in a 2-1 victory at Carlisle United on 9 January 1993. City went on to win the Third Division and the Welsh Cup.

## WORLD CUP BLUEBIRDS

Four Cardiff City players were in the Wales squad that reached the quarter-finals of the 1958 World Cup Tournament in Sweden. Derek Sullivan played against Hungary and Sweden in the opening group stages, against Hungary in the group play-off, and against Brazil in the quarter-final. Colin Baker played against Mexico in the group stages. Ron Hewitt played against Sweden in the group stages, against Hungary in the group play-off, and against Brazil in the quarter-final. Ken Jones was the reserve goalkeeper, but did not play in any of Wales's five matches.

## SELF-CATERING IN GEORGIA

When Cardiff City travelled to Georgia in late September 1977 for a European Cup Winners' Cup first-round second-leg tie against Dynamo Tblisi, the club were advised to take their own food for the players to avoid any potential problems which might arise from eating the local Georgian food. So City took their own food with them: 144 lamb chops, 72 steaks, 180 eggs, 200 pats of butter, 192 packets of breakfast cereals, 400 tea-bags, 20 loaves of bread, 7lbs of marmalade, 7lbs of lump sugar, 7lbs of mashed potatoes, 72 chocolate bars, 4lbs of margarine, 7lbs of peas, oranges, and enough powdered milk to make up 14 gallons. The players may have been better off risking the local cheese pie speciality – they lost the tie 3-0 in front of a 100,000 attendance, and went out of the competition on a 3-1 aggregate.

## NEWSPAPER CORRESPONDENTS

*The South Wales Echo's* Saturday night *Football Echo* began publication on the resumption of peacetime football in August 1919 after the First World War. The main football correspondents covering Cardiff City in the *Football Echo* until it ceased publication in 2005 have been:

| Name | Date |
| --- | --- |
| E L Jobbins | (1919-25) |
| Harry Ditton | (1925-35) |
| Dewi Lewis | (1946-52) |
| Jim Hill | (1952-58) |
| Mervyn Thomas | (1958-60) |
| Peter Corrigan | (1960-63) |
| Brian Styles | (1963-65) |
| Peter Jackson | (1965-74) |
| Joe Lovejoy | (1974-85) |
| Martyn Bedford | (1985-87) |
| Robert Phillips | (1987-97) |
| Terry Phillips | (1997-2005) |

Jobbins, Ditton and Lewis were also at various times 'Citizen' of *The Western Mail*. One other newspaper that covered Cardiff City was the *South Wales Daily News*, a rival publication to *The Western Mail*. The football correspondent of the SWDN was Arthur "Arthurian" Stephens, who covered Cardiff City from the club's inception as a professional side in 1910 until 1928, when the paper merged with *The Western Mail*.

## LIGHTING UP

It was not until the summer of 1960, following Cardiff City's promotion to the old Division One, that floodlights were installed at Ninian Park, City being one of the last League clubs to be lit up. The lights were first used for the home match against Sheffield Wednesday on 24 August 1960, but were officially opened with a friendly match against Zurich Grasshoppers on 5 October of that year.

## THE DETACHABLE COLLAR

Cardiff City's midfield player Malcolm Clarke (1967-69) was well known as a smart dresser, and would wear detachable shirt-collars on matchdays. On one occasion, City defender Brian Harris, always the dressing-room joker, had obtained a smaller-size collar and swapped it for Clarke's usual collar while he was in the bath after a match. When Clarke tried to fasten the 'new' collar, he almost choked himself – much to the amusement of Harris and his City team-mates!

## DISASTROUS RUN

Cardiff City last played at the top level in 1961/62, and when they defeated Sheffield Wednesday 2-1 at Ninian Park on 11 November 1961, the Bluebirds were in a comfortable seventh place after seventeen games. But they could win only once in their next 21 matches, and were relegated despite winning two and drawing one of their final four matches – too little, too late!

## MERRETT'S TAKEOVER

A takeover battle for Cardiff City was on the move by March 1939, with Cardiff industrialist H H (later Sir Herbert) Merrett having acquired a large shareholding and offering to relieve the board of directors of their liabilities. But despite having waited outside the directors' weekly meeting at the Park Hotel on several occasions, Mr Merrett could not gain an interview with them. City were then a mid-table Third Division (South) side with encouraging attendances, but there seemed to be no concrete ambition to regain a top-level place. After enlisting the support of the local press, Mr Merrett duly gained a place on the board, and became chairman in April 1939. He immediately appointed a new manager in Cyril Spiers, who had been the assistant at Wolverhampton Wanderers. Despite the outbreak of war in September 1939, City built a wartime side of local youngsters, and when peacetime League football restarted in 1946, Merrett and Spiers took City back to the top level within five years.

## EVANS STAYED IN GERMANY

Cardiff City's first professional signing Jack Evans volunteered for service in World War I, but his recruitment grouping meant that he was able to play for the Bluebirds on a regular basis until March 1916. He was to remain in the Forces until April 1919 because, although the war ended with the Armistice of November 1918, he was then sent to join the Allied Occupation Army stationed in a defeated Germany.

## OVER THE BAR

The first-ever penalty shoot-out in which Cardiff City took part was in the European Cup Winners' Cup first round second leg match against Dynamo Berlin at Ninian Park on 29 September 1971. The first leg had finished 1-1, as did the second match after extra time. The tie went to penalties, and City skipper Don Murray put the Bluebirds' second spot-kick over the bar at the Grange End. City lost the shoot-out 4-5.

## AMATEUR ACHIEVEMENTS BY EVANS

Llandaff-born wing-half Herbie Evans was a Wales Schools international before World War One and also played for Cardiff Corinthians. He joined Cardiff City as an amateur in the summer of 1920, and as such played a number of times in Second and First Division football as well as representing Wales at amateur level and in the professional side. Evans, who worked for Cardiff Docks firm Llewellyn, Merrett & Price, eventually turned professional with Cardiff City in late March 1922.

## 'TRANSFER' FROM BOLTON

A Cardiff City 'signing' from Bolton Wanderers was first seen at Ninian Park on 8 February 2002. The giant TV screen in the Popular Bank/Grange End corner had been bought from Wanderers, who had used it at their old Burnden Park ground before they moved to the Reebok Stadium.

## OPPONENTS FAILED TO SHOW

During the first half of the 1915/16 season, with the Southern League disbanded at the end of 1914/15 for the duration of the War, Cardiff City played friendly matches until taking part in the South-West Combination from January to April 1916. One of the friendlies – against Southampton at Ninian Park on 20 November 1915 – had to be called off at the last minute because of the non-arrival of the opposition. They had left Southampton by train in ample time to reach Cardiff for a 2pm kick-off. But owing to the movement of troop trains in Hampshire, they were delayed at Salisbury. They hired taxis to take them to Bristol, but missed the only possible train connection to Cardiff by just a few minutes. With spectators already at Ninian Park, a blackboard was carried around the pitch showing the message 'Match off – Southampton unable to reach Cardiff'. Most of the fans asked for their money back and left, but 1000 stayed behind to see City play a hurriedly-arranged game against a Welsh Field Ambulance Team.

## GILES'S WELSH QUARTET

Former Welsh international David Giles, who joined Cardiff City as an apprentice in the early 1970s after leaving school, became the only player to appear with four Welsh clubs in the Football League. He was with Cardiff City, Wrexham, Swansea City and Newport County, and also played for Birmingham City, Leyton Orient (loan) and Crystal Palace.

## BLUEBIRDS HAD TO WALK

When Cardiff City travelled to Leicester City for their FA Cup Second Round (now Fourth Round) match on 23 February 1923, they travelled by train from Cardiff and were met at Leicester station by a charabanc (an open single-decker coach of that period) which was to take them to Leicester's Filbert Street ground. But the crowds in the vicinity were so dense that the charabanc could not get through. The driver had to stop half a mile from Filbert Street and the players had to walk, with trainer George Latham and the directors pushing the kit basket!

## SWEET REVENGE

On 3 September 1955, Cardiff City were beaten 9-1 at Ninian Park by Wolverhampton Wanderers in a First Division game, a result that equalled a 47-year-old record away win in that division. City's goal was scored when they were 9-0 down, by Ron Stockin, whom they had signed from Wolves twelve months earlier. On 31 December 1955, City went to Molineux for the return match, and a large Press contingent turned up expecting to see another drubbing for City. But the Bluebirds, in the lower half of the table, were all-out for revenge, and beat well-placed Wolves 2-0 with goals from Gerry Hitchens and Trevor Ford. It was Wolves' first home defeat of that season!

## FIRST BLUEBIRDS' SUB

Substitutes for matches were first introduced for season 1965/66. It was one substitute per team, and he could only be used as an injury replacement. Cardiff City's first League substitute appeared on 21 August 1965, in the opening game of the season against Bury at Ninian Park, when David Summerhayes came on for the injured Colin Baker.

## FIRST TIME TOP

Cardiff City reached the summit of the Football League for the first time in September 1923 when, after winning three and drawing one of their opening four matches, they went top of the original Division One, remaining there for most of the season. Only four years earlier, City had been in the Southern League.

## DESERTED BOB BANK

When Cardiff City kicked off in their Third Division (South) home match against Queens Park Rangers on 14 November 1931, there was not a solitary spectator on the Bob Bank or in the Grand Stand, and there were less than 2000 in the ground. Some more did turn up, but the eventual 3491 crowd had to endure a 0-4 home defeat.

# A TV SIGNING

When Cardiff City bought England 'B' left-winger Derek Hogg from West Bromwich Albion on Thursday 27 October 1960 for a fee of £12,000, the actual signing took place that evening on a local television weekly sports programme, *Sports Preview*, broadcast by the independent Welsh station TWW, forerunner of HTV. Hogg made his Bluebirds debut the following night at Ninian Park against Leicester City, one of his former clubs, and scored in the Bluebirds' 2-1 win.

# A STATELY HOME MATCH

At the end of the 1952/53 season, First Division Cardiff City were invited to play Third Division (South) Champions Bristol Rovers in aid of the National Playing Fields Association and the King George VI Memorial Fund. The match took place on Monday 4 May 1953 in Badminton Park, Gloucestershire, on the estate of His Grace The Duke of Beaufort. A pitch was laid out in the park with temporary stands, and a 12,000 attendance saw City beaten 3-1 by Rovers. After the game, the two teams, club officials and their wives were guests of the Duke and Duchess at a buffet supper served in one of the magnificent state rooms of Badminton House.

# FORD REFUSED TO PLAY

Bluebirds' Welsh international centre-forward Trevor Ford was recalled by secretary/manager Trevor Morris to face Birmingham after a few matches in the reserves. Ford was selected at inside-left, but gave his manager notice that he would refuse to play in that role. On the afternoon of the match, on 26 November 1955, Ford arrived at Ninian Park to be told that he would have to play at inside-left. He still refused, and left the ground before the game, which Cardiff won 2-1. As a result, the directors suspended him without pay for a period of 14 days for what they described as "a flagrant breach of discipline". Ford, however, did not lose out financially, as he sold his story to a national newspaper for a sum equal to the amount of his lost wages.

## EVANS THE FOOTBALLING PRINTER

Cardiff City's first-ever professional signing Jack Evans was by trade a printer's compositor. He worked on a part-time basis for the club's printers - the Imperial Printing Company of Cardiff, one of whose directors was former Riverside player Ivor Parker, who was on City's first board of directors. Welsh-speaking Evans was involved regularly in the printing of City's match programme, which the firm produced. Following his retirement as a player, having spent the final two years of his career – 1926-28 – with Bristol Rovers, Evans continued in the printing trade until the mid 1950s, when he retired. He continued to attend matches at Ninian Park for many years.

## A NEW HAT, PLEASE

At the start of 1910/11, Cardiff City's first season at Ninian Park, there was bench seating at each end for spectators from corner-flag to corner-flag, inside the fencing around the pitch. It was a risky place to sit, and one supporter had his straw boater-hat smashed to pieces by a wayward shot from City's Bob Peake. The fan came to the dressing room after the final whistle to demand compensation from the player, but he left empty-handed with what remained of his hat.

## DIRECTORS JOINED UP

First World War hostilities began in early August 1914, but there was no enforced conscription until 1916, prior to which there was volunteer recruitment. Cardiff City's match programme for 6 February 1915 stated that nine of the club's playing-staff had volunteered up to that time, the most recent recruits being half-back Fred Keenor and goalkeeper Jack Stephenson, who had both enlisted in the 17th Middlesex Regiment, popularly known as the 'Footballers' Battalion'. They were not required to report until called upon to do so, and were therefore available to continue playing. A few weeks later, two of City's directors – Doctor William Nicholson and Mr Frederick Schroeter – also joined the Army. Doctor Nicholson served in the Medical Corps while Mr Schroeter joined the 63rd Infantry Brigade to train as a transport driver.

## THE HYPNOTIST

Bluebirds' defender Bert Smith, an Irish international, claimed that he could hypnotise opponents. When Cardiff and Sunderland met at Ninian Park on 3 December 1921, the Cardiff players asked Sunderland's England international Charlie Buchan to act as though he was hypnotised by Smith. City won 2-0, though Buchan in his autobiography states that he was unaffected. But the 'influence' certainly failed the following Saturday in the return match at Roker Park, when Sunderland were 4-1 winners. A few weeks later, City players were in Canton when Smith claimed that he could stop a tram by hypnotising the driver. He stood in the middle of the tramlines and stared at the driver as the oncoming tram came from the direction of Victoria Park. It stopped alright – it had to, otherwise Smith would have been run down!

## AN INFAMOUS DEBUT FOR BATER

Ely-born Phil Bater was signed from Brentford in July 1987. He made his debut in the Fourth Division at Wrexham on 12 September 1987, but was sent off in the first half for a second bookable offence – the only Cardiff City player to date to be dismissed on his debut.

## A SEASON TO FORGET!

When Cardiff City finished at the bottom of Division Three (South) in 1933/34, they were beaten no fewer than 27 times in their 42 League matches. And goals were conceded by the hatful – the Bluebirds let in 105!

## ON CAME THE HORSES

Ninian Park has on two occasions staged show-jumping on the pitch. In the summer of 1958, when the Empire Games were staged in Cardiff, the Games' show-jumping Championships were held at the ground, while in May 1960 the Hobby Horse Championships were also held there; which was a trial event to select the team for the Rome Olympics of that year.

## LITERARY BLUEBIRD

One of Cardiff City's longest-serving supporters is Cardiff-born author, poet and playwright Dr Dannie Abse who has been watching the club since 1933/34. He is one of Britain's leading literary names, and his careers in medicine and writing ran in parallel. Dannie sometimes used the names of City players in his works, among them Eli Postin (1933/34), Albert Keating (1930/31-32/33) and his brother Reg (1933/34-35/36) who live on in Dannie's novel *Some Corner Of An English Field*.

## MIDNIGHT TRANSFER

The £12,000 transfer of Welsh international winger George Edwards from Birmingham to Cardiff City took place just before midnight on Friday 11 December 1948, with Cardiff due to play at Leicester the next day. At that time, the deadline for pre-match registrations with the Football League was midnight, and manager Cyril Spiers rushed to George's lodgings to complete the deal. George got out of bed to meet City's boss, and was in his pyjamas and dressing-gown when he signed. He made his Bluebirds debut at Filbert Street in a 2-2 draw just hours later. During his playing career with the Bluebirds, George, who had gained his BA degree at Swansea University during the early part of the war, went on to gain an MA degree from Birmingham University – a rare achievement for a professional footballer in those days. His thesis on the Pembrokeshire coalfields still remains an essential reference-work for geology students. George went into the retail oil-company business towards the end of his playing career, dealing in fuel supplies to firms in the South Wales and West area. He made his final appearance for Cardiff City at the age of 34 in a Football Combination match against Norwich City on 4 May 1955. He was also a journalist with a weekly football column in the *Wales Sunday Empire News*, and a BBC radio and television Welsh region football reporter on their Saturday evening round-up programmes. In addition he became a Cardiff City director for many years, and a local magistrate, as well as serving on the Sports Council of Wales and Football Association of Wales tribunals.

## WILLIAMS OF WEMBLEY

Former Cardiff City skipper Gareth Williams was as Welsh as they come. He was from the Rhondda, and was signed as a junior player in June 1961, eventually moving to Bolton Wanderers for a £45,000 fee in October 1967. But he could never play for Wales, as he had been born at a Wembley hospital in October 1941 while his mother was in north-west London visiting his father, who was employed on vital wartime work. In the mid 1970s, after Gareth had retired, the rules were changed to allow sons of Welsh parents to play for Wales.

## NETS NOT SECURED

When City equalised at the Grange End, 15 minutes from the end of a 1-1 draw with Crystal Palace on 23 January 1937, the ball went under the net, which was not properly secured. Palace players appealed for a goal-kick, and their goalkeeper Vince Lore placed the ball on the edge of his six-yard box. But referee G S Blackhall of Wednesbury had given a goal, and carried the ball back to the centre-spot. Palace players gave up their protest and accepted the decision. Their goal 15 minutes earlier at the Canton End had also gone under the net – someone on City's ground-staff had presumably not secured the nets properly before the game!

## A LUCKY FIND

When City's players were on the Royal Birkdale golf course at Southport in February 1927, whilst in training for their FA Cup fifth round tie at Bolton, they were followed round the course on several occasions by a small black kitten from one of the houses bordering the links. The players saw this as a lucky omen, and sent centre-forward Hughie Ferguson to find the kitten's owner. He duly did so, and it was agreed that if the players could keep the kitten, then they would supply its owner with a Cup Final ticket if they reached Wembley. The kitten, which they named Trixie, did indeed prove to be a lucky mascot, and City went on to win the FA Cup. Trixie remained with the club until she died in 1939.

## ONE FOR ALL

When Ninian Park was officially opened on 1 September 1910, there were no separate dressing rooms for the home team and the visitors. Both sides used one single room and washing facilities until the start of the 1913/14 season, when the club installed separate quarters for each team... and separate baths!

## RUGBY LEAGUE ATTEMPT

Following Cardiff City's departures at the end of 1980/81 from the Football Combination (voted out) and Welsh League (resigned), the club decided to run a Rugby League side to play in the League's Second Division. The Cardiff Blue Dragons started promisingly in terms of support, with over 9000 at Ninian Park to see the opening match against Salford on 30 August 1981, when Salford were 26-21 winners. But the Blue Dragons lasted just three seasons, during which time attendances gradually fell to below 1000. In addition, the Ninian Park pitch was badly affected. The Blue Dragons were put into liquidation in the summer of 1984 by Cardiff City's owners Kenton Utilities and moved to Bridgend to play under a new name. The whole operation had cost City £140,000, and the Blue Dragons lost between £5000 and £7000 in each season of their existence.

## CAVIAR FOR THE CHAIRMAN

Bluebirds chairman Stefan Terlezski could not accompany the club to Georgia in late September 1977 for their European Cup Winners' Cup first round second leg tie against Dynamo Tblisi because of his political activities with the Conservative Party. Georgia was then part of the USSR, and it was feared that he may be detained by the Soviet authorities, as he had originally come to Britain from the Ukraine in the immediate post-war years. But in his absence from the match, Dynamo Tblisi sent back a few gifts for him with Cardiff City – he received two kilos of caviar, several bottles of vodka, 14 bottles of Georgian wine, and two bottles of Georgian brandy. It was some consolation for City's defeat.

## EARNIE'S RECORD-BREAKING GOAL

Robert Earnshaw's equaliser at Crewe on 3 May 2003 was his 31st League goal of that season and beat the club record of 30 League goals, recorded by Stan Richards in 1946/47. Ernie also scored four Cup goals to take his season's League and Cup total to 35. No other player has ever scored that many for the Bluebirds over the course of a season.

## 'THE AYATOLLAH'

The action of Cardiff City fans in tapping their heads with their hands in unison during matches has its origins in the televised scenes of mourning during the early 1990s at the funeral in Tehran of Iran's spiritual leader Ayatollah Khomeini whose followers beat their heads in despair at his passing. For reasons best known to themselves, Bluebirds fans adopted the practice, and still do it to this day. New players are informed of it by their colleagues, and do the same when acknowledging the crowd. Even former City players in opposition have been known to do it!

## DISASTROUS DEBUTS

Two Cardiff City players made their first-team debuts for the club in 7-1 defeats. Full-back Gary Bell, signed from Lower Gornal in February 1966, conceded two penalties in the 7-1 defeat at Wolves on 21 September that year. Defender Brian Harris, signed from Everton on 14 October 1966, made his debut in the 7-1 defeat at Plymouth on the following day. The previous May, Harris had been named man-of-the-match in Everton's FA Cup Final 3-2 victory over Sheffield Wednesday at Wembley.

## WELSH CUP CONSISTENCY

From May 1967 to May 1971, Cardiff City won five consecutive Welsh Cup Finals. During that time they were unbeaten in 28 ties. The run eventually came to an end in May 1972, when City lost the first leg of the Final, Wrexham beating them 2-1. By then City had totalled 31 ties without defeat.

## GRANGE END OPENED

The Lord Mayor of Cardiff – Alderman A J Howell JP – attended the Cardiff City v Burnley match on 1 September 1928 and officially declared open the newly-built Grange End covered stand, which replaced the earth bank behind that goal. He used silver scissors to cut a blue and white ribbon stretched between the centre stanchions of the new stand, which accommodated 18,000 under cover. It was built by Cardiff firm Connies & Meaden Limited on Dumballs Road, and stood for fifty years until its demolition for safety reasons in the first six months of 1978. The Cardiff v Burnley match was City's opening home game of that season, and they celebrated the occasion by winning 7-0, with Hughie Ferguson scoring five goals. But the Bluebirds netted only 35 more goals in their remaining forty matches, and were relegated!

## FLIGHT POSTPONED

Cardiff City were due to make their first-ever flight on 4 March 1946, when they were scheduled to leave RAF St Athan for Germany on a Dakota transport aircraft to play a British Army of the Rhine team in Dusseldorf two days later. The match had been arranged at the request of Field Marshal Montgomery who had been asked by Welsh soldiers in his command if he could use his influence in getting the Bluebirds to come to Germany. But the flight was cancelled because of bad weather, and it was a month later that City were able to play a BAOR side in Braunschweig, drawing 1-1.

## GETTING THE GAS AND WATER

When Secretary/Manager Fred Stewart arrived from Stockport County in May 1911 he took it upon himself to have gas and water connected to the club office and communal dressing room. The club's board of directors duly endorsed his action, and from 15 August 1911 the players were allowed to have hot baths after matches at Ninian Park, instead of using bowls of water heated on a coal-fired stove.

## TWO BUS RIDES FOR THE CUP

Although Cardiff City have only won the FA Cup on one occasion, it has been paraded twice around the city – eighty years apart! On Monday 25 April 1927, two days after the win against Arsenal, the trophy was taken in triumph by the players, on their return from London, from Cardiff General Station to the City Hall in an open charabanc. In April 2007, the same trophy followed the same route on an open-top City Sightseeing bus as part of an S4C television documentary to mark the eightieth anniversary of the Bluebirds' victory.

## MASSIVE FINE FOR DAVE BENNETT

After City had missed a number of chances in a 3-2 defeat at Plymouth on 28 December 1982, including one when winger Dave Bennett shot wide from a narrow angle instead of centring the ball to unmarked Bob Hatton, manager Len Ashurst made it known to the press that he would fine Bennett for being selfish. The publicity carried on for several days. Bennett thought that he would be fined a substantial amount, but it was a case of Ashurst being clever – he fined Bennett the massive sum of £1! The lesson was learned, and Bennett's contribution from the wing was a vital factor in City's promotion.

## WE CAN SEE YOU!

In early April 1990, *South Wales Echo* football correspondent Robert Phillips was officially banned by Cardiff City from Ninian Park as a reporter following his criticism of the way chairman Tony Clemo handled the Bluebirds' affairs. But the intrepid reporter managed to watch matches from the Popular Bank, disguised in a flat cap and dark glasses. Club stewards knew perfectly well who he was, but his appearance fooled them. The ban lasted until club benefactor Rick Wright became involved with City towards the end of the 1990/91 season. It was not the first time that a *South Wales Echo* football correspondent had been banned – Peter Corrigan (in the early 1960s), Peter Jackson (early 1970s) and Joe Lovejoy (late 1970s) had all suffered similar fates.

## JUST IN TIME

Cardiff City goalkeeper Ken Jones, who joined the Bluebirds from Aberdare local football in 1953 after leaving school, made his City debut in November 1957 and established a regular place during the remainder of that season. On Wednesday, 26 March 1958, he was at home watching the televised FA Cup semi-final replay at Highbury between Fulham and Manchester United, a match that kicked off in mid-afternoon. During the second half, he suddenly realised that he should have been at Ninian Park for City's Second Division game against Bristol Rovers that was to kick off at 5pm. Jones raced to the ground and arrived ten minutes before kick-off, with Graham Vearncombe about to take his place. But Jones played in City's 0-2 defeat that day, though he was dropped for the next game as a disciplinary measure by the club's secretary/manager Trevor Morris. He played in the Welsh League side that Saturday at Haverfordwest, and scored from a penalty in City's 2-1 win… though in so doing he burst the ball! At the end of that season, Jones went with Wales to the World Cup Finals in Sweden as reserve goalkeeper to Arsenal's Jack Kelsey.

## STEWART'S COSTLY ERROR

Following the transfer in mid-January 1930 of winger Freddy Warren, full-back Jack Jennings and goalkeeper Joe Hillier from Cardiff City to Middlesbrough, it was agreed by City's secretary/manager Fred Stewart, acting on behalf of his board, that the north-east club would pay a further £250 when both Jennings and Hillier had played 20 League games for Boro. But when City asked for their extra money in May 1933, Middlesbrough sent only £50, and said that was the figure agreed by Stewart with the Boro secretary two years earlier. Stewart had resigned from his position with City in May 1933, but was asked to attend a board meeting a month later to clarify the situation. He explained that he had unaccountably written £50 in his letter to Middlesbrough in January 1930, and not £250! He said that he was prepared to swear on oath that he had verbally agreed by telephone a figure of £250. But the Football League ruled in favour of Middlesbrough, and City lost out on £200 – a considerable sum in those days – because of Stewart's error.

## SIX ABSENT, BUT BLUEBIRDS WON!

Prior to the 1970s, clubs were not allowed to request a postponement of their League fixture, however many of their players were absent on international duty. On Saturday 14 April 1923, Cardiff City were at home to Sheffield United in a First Division game with six of their regular side playing for their respective countries in the Home International Championship that day. Jimmy Blair played for Scotland against England at Hampden Park, while in the Wales v Ireland match at Wrexham, Fred Keenor, Len Davies and Jack Evans were in the Welsh line-up, and Tom Farquharson and Bert Smith played for Ireland. Back at Ninian Park, a depleted Cardiff City, with six reserves, beat Sheffield United 1-0.

## THIRTEEN-GOAL THRILLER!

After a disappointing first half of season 1925/26, the Bluebirds were looking forward to improved fortunes in the new year. But when they went to Sheffield United on 1 January, they lost 11-2. It was City's heaviest-ever League defeat – Happy New Year!

## KEEPING POSSESSION

Following the termination of manager Cyril Spiers' contract in May 1954, Cardiff City asked him for possession of the club house in St Malo Road, Heath, Cardiff, which Spiers was occupying. He refused to move out until he found another managerial job. The club threatened legal action, but Spiers stayed on. He was appointed Crystal Palace manager in September 1954, but even then did not move out for another two months.

## BLUEBIRDS HIT MARK FOR NINE!

*South Wales Echo* football reporter Mark Bloom played in Welsh League football in his younger days, and once played against Cardiff City's first team. It was at Ninian Park on 5 December 1992 when the Bluebirds met Caerau in the fourth round of the Welsh Cup. He came on for Caerau as substitute – and his side lost 9-0!

## O'HALLORAN'S HAT-TRICK DEBUT

Many players have scored on their Cardiff City debuts, but only one has netted a hat-trick on his first senior appearance for the club. Part-timer Neil O'Halloran, who worked in Cardiff docks as a boilermaker, did so in a 3-1 home win against Charlton Athletic on 10 December 1955, but never established himself in the side as a regular first-team player. He made only ten League appearances for City before moving to Newport County in the summer of 1957. He later played for Merthyr Tydfil and Barry Town before becoming a successful engineering contractor. He eventually became chairman and owner, together with his wife Paula, of Barry Town.

## PLAYED AND MANAGED

Four men have played for and managed Cardiff City. Davy McDougall was player/manager in 1910/11. Alan Durban was a player from 1958 to 1963, and was manager from September 1984 to May 1986. Richie Morgan was a player from 1966 to 1978, and manager from 1978 to 1981. Russell Osman was a player in 1995/96, and manager from 11 November to 24 December 1996.

## DRESSING ROOM SWITCH

It was an injury reshuffle in a Second Division match against Hull City at Ninian Park on 11 November 1950 that was the foundation of the Bluebirds winning promotion to Division One in the following season, 1951/52. City were losing to Hull 1-0 at half time, with right-half Bobby McLaughlin struggling with an injury. Manager Cyril Spiers was away on a scouting mission, and during the interval chairman Sir Herbert Merrett went to the home dressing room to see what the coaching staff and players were going to do about the situation. A discussion between Merrett and the staff led to a reshuffle that saw right-winger Wilf Grant being switched to centre-forward. City won the game 2-1, and Grant did so well in his new role that he kept his place and became top scorer that season, when the club narrowly missed going up. He again led City's scoring chart the following year, when they returned to top-level football for the first time since 1929.

## NEARLY GOT AWAY WITH IT!

When Cardiff City played Bristol City at Ashton Gate in a Second Division match on 16 January 1960, Bluebirds former Arsenal forward Derek Tapscott hit a fierce shot inches wide. The ball hit the goal stanchion and flew back onto the pitch. Tapscott knew it was wide, but ran back to the centre-circle celebrating with team-mate Graham Moore as if it were a goal. Unfortunately for them, the referee had spotted it, and gave a goal-kick. Bluebirds won the game 3-0.

## A 'HEADED' PENALTY!

Cardiff City full-back Gary Bell is the only player in the club's history to have headed a goal as a result of a penalty. On 29 September 1973 in the Second Division game against Hull City at Ninian Park, Gary took a penalty at the Grange End four minutes before half-time, and saw his effort parried into the air by Hull keeper Jeff Wealands. As the ball looped up, Gary headed it into the net. Up to that time, only five players had done that, including England internationals Eddie Hapgood (Arsenal) and Bill 'Dixie' Dean (Everton). City lost the game 3-1.

## THE SOURCE OF THE NICKNAME

A play performed in November 1911 at Cardiff's New Theatre led to Cardiff City being nicknamed The Bluebirds. The play, by Belgian author Maurice Maeterlinck, was 'The Blue Bird', and the theme of it was that children were trying to imprison The Blue Bird, a symbol of happiness, in a cage. Maeterlinck's point was that happiness cannot be imprisoned, and is there for everyone to partake of it. Shortly after the end of the play's run at the New Theatre, Maeterlinck was awarded the Nobel Prize for Literature for his various works. There was a considerable amount of publicity in the local press as the play had just left Cardiff, and supporters of Cardiff City, then in their second professional season, began calling their blue-shirted team The Blue Birds, the name gradually being shortened to Bluebirds.

## ORIENT'S BLUEBIRDS SOUVENIR

Following the Bluebirds' election to Division Two of the Football League on 31 May 1920, the first-ever League match played at Ninian Park was against Clapton (now Leyton) Orient three months later. It ended 0-0 in front of a 25,000 attendance, and to mark the occasion City's directors presented their Orient counterparts with a framed illustrated address on vellum. It bore the inscription: 'Presented to Clapton Orient FC by the directors of Cardiff City FC as a memento of the first English League match played in Wales.' The inscription also included the names of all the players who took part in the game, and a list of directors of both clubs.

## BARKING MAD?

Former Middlesbrough forward Billy Woof had been signed on a trial contract by manager Len Ashurst, and was included in the side to face Wigan on 11 September 1982 because of an injury to Jeff Hemmerman. Woof scored the winner in a 3-2 victory, but was angry on the Monday when told that Hemmerman would return in his place for the midweek League Cup first round second leg match against Hereford United. Woof walked out, and remains the only player in Cardiff City's history to have scored in every first-team game that he played for the club – all one of them!

## A REMARKABLE PENALTY SAVE

In their FA Cup Sixth Round replay at Ninian Park on 9 March 1927, City's Irish international keeper Tom Farquharson made a remarkable first-half penalty save when City led 2-0. Defending the Canton End goal, Farquharson retreated into the net, and as Chelsea's Andy Wilson started his approach to the ball, Farquharson advanced to his goal-line. The rule at the time was that, for a penalty, the goalkeeper could not advance beyond his line until the ball was kicked. At the instant that Wilson made contact with the ball, Farquharson's momentum was such that he smothered the shot on his six-yard line! So many keepers copied the move that two years later FIFA changed the rules to require the keeper to stand still on his line until the ball was kicked.

## WAKE MISSED OUT ON CUP WINNERS' MEDAL

Cardiff City's 1925 FA Cup Final 1-0 defeat by Sheffield United was due to an error by Bluebirds right-half Harry Wake. He was caught in possession by United winger Fred Tunstall, who easily scored. Two years later, ex-Newcastle United player Wake scored in City's 3-0 FA Cup semi-final win over Reading. He was all set for Wembley and Arsenal, and the opportunity to make up for 1925, but on 16 April 1927, seven days before the Final, he suffered a bad blow to his kidneys in the 3-2 home win over Sheffield Wednesday and was detained in Cardiff Royal Infirmary. One national newspaper mistakenly reported that he had died! He was out in time to go with City's official party to Wembley, but was unfit for selection and so missed out on a winner's medal. Wake was with City from 1923 until 1931, when he joined Mansfield Town. In the early 1950s, he made a nostalgic visit to Ninian Park and described his eight years with the Bluebirds "the happiest time of my life".

## CHANGING TRAINS

Cardiff City half-back Jack 'Ginger' Lewis, who lived in Newport, was due to play for the Bluebirds at Aston Villa on 31 October 1925. As he was about to join his team-mates on the train at Newport for the journey to Birmingham, he was told not to travel and to catch a train to Cardiff where he would make his international debut for Wales against Scotland at Ninian Park. Late withdrawals from the Welsh team had resulted in his selection the previous night, but Lewis had no telephone at home, and could not be contacted.

## TWO GREAT RECOVERIES

In the space of three days, Cardiff City came from behind in two consecutive matches at Ninian Park to score late in the game and win on each occasion. On 23 November 2000, they defeated Lincoln City 3-2 after being 2-1 down with a couple of minutes left. Two days later, they did the same again, this time beating Hartlepool United 3-2.

## A WET WELCOME

When Cardiff City's players reached their dressing room after their 4-0 defeat at Brighton on 29 October 1977, they found all their clothes floating in the bath. Robin Friday, sent off in the second half, had done the deed and then left the ground. His team-mates had to travel home to South Wales wearing tracksuits and training footwear borrowed from Brighton.

## OUT IN THE COLD

At the start of the 1980/81 season, Cardiff City fielded reserve sides in the Football Combination and the Welsh League, having played in both competitions over a near sixty-year period, but at the end of that season they were out of both leagues. They resigned from the Welsh League as they did not consider the standard good enough for their young players, but then found themselves out of the Football Combination, having finished second from bottom and failing to gain re-election at the Combination's Annual General Meeting. The Bluebirds have not since competed in either League.

## COME WITH US, PLEASE

When Cardiff City travelled by road to play Northampton Town in Division Two on 15 February 1964, a police car halted the team-coach at Chepstow. A police officer boarded the coach and asked if there was a Mr Derek Tapscott with the team. City's former Welsh international was then asked to leave the coach by the police, and was immediately taken back to Cardiff. But it was not an arrest – Tappy's wife Glenys had gone into labour. She was taken to hospital, and gave birth to their second daughter later that day.

## SIX FOR, THEN SIX AGAINST!

When Cardiff City played at Preston North End in Division Two on 29 September 1962, they won 6-2 in what was their biggest win of that season. A week later, on 6 October, the Bluebirds went to Chelsea and lost 6-0 in what was their biggest defeat of that season.

## RAF LEAVE

Tremorfa-born half-back Colin Baker was with Cardiff City from 1952, when he joined the club as an amateur, to 1965/66 when he retired. He continued with the club until 1973, on the commercial side in which he had been involved for the last few years of his playing career. Welsh international Colin had made his first-team debut in the final First Division game of 1953/54, when he played in a 2-2 draw against Sheffield Wednesday at Ninian Park on 24 April 1954. At the time he was doing his National Service in the RAF and was a part-timer with City. He was given special leave to make his debut by his Commanding Officer, and he did not become a full-time professional until mid-March 1955, a few weeks after being released from the RAF.

## AND THE ROOF FELL IN!

A 51,656 official attendance packed Ninian Park for the Third Division (South) match between leaders Cardiff City and Bristol City on 7 April 1947. Two fans had climbed onto the pitched roof of the Grange End covered terrace to get a good view of the game. They edged their way down to the front guttering, and one of them fell through the roof! Those underneath heard the corrugated sheets start to break, and managed to cushion the fall of the foolhardy fan. He was unhurt, but was taken to St David's Hospital suffering from bruises and shock. The hole was repaired, but the patch was for many years a reminder to City fans of what had happened that day.

## DOUBLE BREAK

Bluebirds wing-half Glyn Williams joined the club in August 1946, when he was signed from local Caerau football. He journeyed with Cardiff City from their Division Three (South) days of 1946/47 to Division One at the end of 1951/52, but after being a regular in City's line-up in the first few months of 1952/53, he broke his leg in a 2-0 win at Chelsea on 8 November 1952. He was on his way to recovery, but in mid-March 1953 fell over at his home, and broke the same leg once more. He never played League football again, and joined Aberystwyth Town as player/coach in August 1955.

## AND THE NETS CAUGHT FIRE!

Cardiff City were due to play York City in an FA Cup third round replay at Ninian Park on 6 January 1970, but the goalmouths were frozen solid due to the severe cold. Manager Jimmy Scoular borrowed a garden flame-gun in an effort to thaw the ground, but was making little progress in his use of it, apart from scorching the pitch. When someone shouted to him that he was wanted on the telephone, he turned around – and set the creosoted goalnet on fire! The game was, in any event, postponed because of the icy pitch.

## RUGBY UNION AT NINIAN PARK

Cardiff RFC played Bristol RFC under lights at Ninian Park on Tuesday 14 March 1961, before floodlighting had been installed at Cardiff Arms Park. Cardiff had previously played Bristol under lights at Bristol City's Ashton Gate, and the Ninian Park game had been originally scheduled for 3 November 1960. It was postponed due to bad weather, as was the second attempt on 22 November. On the third occasion, 7000 saw Bristol beat Cardiff 19-14. And on November 15th 1961, the two sides met again at Ninian Park, Bristol winning 20-3. Thirty-eight years later, the Schweppes Cup Final between Swansea and Llanelli was also played at Ninian Park, Swansea winning 37-10 on 15 May 1999.

## WE SAW RONNIE MOORE SCORE

Liverpool-born Ronnie Moore had been a prolific scorer for Tranmere Rovers when Cardiff City signed him for £110,000 in February 1979. But despite the hard-working Moore's efforts for the Bluebirds, he netted only six goals in 63 League and Cup appearances. In order to change his luck in front of goal, he started carrying a brass number seven from the front door of his home in Rhoose, and also he began to attend church to pray for a goal. City fans appreciated his efforts, and many supporters wore badges with the logo 'I saw Ronnie Moore Score'. It did not have any effect, but when he joined Rotherham United in August 1980, he helped them to win the Third Division Championship by scoring 23 League goals, with two more in the FA Cup.

## MATCHDAY MORNING SEARCHES

When Ninian Park was officially opened at the start of September 1910, the pitch was very uneven, as it had been laid down on the site of a refuse-tip. When the ground was rolled, stones and glass and so on would work their way to the surface. On matchday mornings, therefore, players, officials, and supporters would walk up and down the pitch in a line looking for offending items. Winger Jack Evans, the club's first-ever professional signing, missed a piece of glass but 'found' it when he fell during the game. He carried the scar on his knee for the rest of his life!

## LEFT SWANS' BOARD TO MANAGE BLUEBIRDS

Cardiff City were struggling in Division Three (South) in 1933/34 and had to seek re-election to the League, finishing at the very bottom just seven years after winning the FA Cup. Secretary-manager Bartley Wilson, who had founded the club as Riverside in 1899, stepped down from team affairs in March 1934 to continue on the administrative side as assistant secretary. His surprise replacement as Bluebirds' manager was Swansea Town director Ben Watts-Jones. An FA of Wales Council member who was in business in Swansea as a draper, Watts-Jones severed his connections with the Swans, with whom he had been since their formation in 1912. He then joined the Bluebirds, and was manager from March 1934 until April 1937, remaining as a director until 1939.

## A PHONE CALL FROM ALEX

Following Cardiff City's success in winning the Championship of Division Three in May 1993, Bluebirds former Manchester United defender Derek Brazil received a phone call at home from "Alex". Thinking that it was someone playing a joke and pretending to be Manchester United manager Alex (now Sir Alex) Ferguson, City's defender uttered a few choice words and put the phone down. Almost immediately the phone rang again, and it was the real Alex Ferguson, with a few choice words of his own before congratulating his former player on a great season with the Bluebirds.

## GROUND IMPROVEMENTS

In the summer of 1992, the main stand seated enclosure was covered by a roof extension, while the area under the covered section of the Popular Bank was raised, with seats being installed along its length. The alterations reduced the ground's capacity to just over 20,000 – a record 62,694 had been present for the Wales v England Home International Championship match in October 1959. Midway through the previous season (1991/92), seats were installed throughout the main stand enclosure. The new facilities, which were first in use on New Year's Day 1992 for the home match with Maidstone United, did not get off to a good start – City lost 5-0 in front of an 8023 attendance.

## PARSONS' ERRORS AFTER PENALTY SAVE

After being a goal down to an unstoppable header from John Hickton in a home match against Middlesbrough on 3 October 1970, Cardiff City took a 3-1 lead through Brian Clark, Bobby Woodruff and Peter King. City goalkeeper Frank Parsons then saved a penalty, but let two soft efforts slip through his hands for Boro to level at 3-3. Parsons could do nothing about Middlesbrough's winner when Hughie McIlmoyle headed in a free-kick late in the game. Parsons, who had been signed in the summer of 1970 from Crystal Palace, didn't play again in the first team that season, and made only one more League appearance for City, at the end of the following season, before joining Fulham.

## RESERVES BEAT SWANS' FIRSTS

With Cardiff City well in the running for promotion to Division One in 1959/60 and due to play a vital game at Leyton Orient, the FA of Wales ordered City to play a Welsh Senior Cup sixth round tie at Swansea two days before their match at Brisbane Road. The Bluebirds protested over the date, but to no avail. They therefore sent a reserve side to the Vetch Field, and beat the Swans' first team 2-1 in an ill-tempered match that saw three players sent off – Steve Mokone and Colin Hudson for City, Harry Griffiths for the Swans.

## DUTIES DIVIDED

From Cardiff City's beginnings as a professional club, the roles of secretary and manager had been combined following the appointment of Fred Stewart in May 1911. But after the resignation of Billy McCandless as Secretary/Manager in November 1947 – he joined Swansea Town – the board decided to introduce separate roles. So former player Trevor Morris, who had been assistant secretary on his return from the RAF after the 1939-45 war, became secretary, while Cyril Spiers, who returned to City in November 1947 after an eighteen-month spell at Norwich City, became manager with sole responsibility for the playing and coaching side of the club.

## A DRAMATIC COLLAPSE

Cardiff City looked well placed for promotion with nine games left after beating Leicester City 3-0 at home on 13 March 1948 in front of 39,000 – but a dramatic collapse saw the Bluebirds' promotion hopes ended. They lost six and drew two of their next eight games, finishing in fourth place. Their home League attendances for that season averaged just under 38,000.

## A WORTHWHILE FINE

Despite the decision of the Football League to expand their numbers and create a new Division Three from the First Division of the Southern League in which Cardiff City had finished fourth in 1919/20, the Bluebirds had decided to seek election directly into the Football League's Second Division. At the Annual General Meeting of the Football League, held at London's Connaught Rooms in the West End on 31 May 1920, City were duly elected, together with Leeds United. The move cost them a fine of £500 from the Southern League for not giving the required notice of withdrawal. City could not have done so in any event, as they could not be 100% certain of their election until it happened. The Bluebirds justified their election and their fine by winning promotion in their very first season as a League club.

## A 21-MATCH UNBEATEN RUN

On 14 September 1946, Cardiff City lost 2-0 at Bournemouth in their sixth League match of the new season. Their record was then three wins and three defeats in Division Three (South). But of their next 21 games, they won 19 and drew two – the best run in the club's history. The sequence ended with a 1-0 defeat at Bristol Rovers on 8 March 1947, and City went on to win promotion and the title.

## THE PLATFORM TICKET

When Reading forward Robin Friday travelled by train to Cardiff to join the Bluebirds on 30 December 1976, he was due to be met at Cardiff General Station by City's kit-man Harry Parsons. But Harry could not find him and, assuming that he would be on the next train, returned to Ninian Park. The club then received a telephone call from British Transport Police at the station, stating that they had detained Friday for travelling on a platform ticket. The club managed to clear up the situation, and Friday was warned by the police about his future conduct. It made little difference to the talented but wildly unpredictable Friday, who caused numerous problems to Cardiff City during his twelve months with the club. He retired from the game after leaving Ninian Park, and was eventually found dead in unexplained circumstances 13 years later at his Ealing flat, a victim of drink and drugs.

## CLOUGH LAID OUT!

Bluebirds skipper Danny Malloy was as tough as they come. A Scotland B international defender who joined City from Dundee in December 1955, he was being riled by Middlesbrough's prolific scorer Brian Clough in a Second Division game at Ayresome Park on 11 January 1958. Eventually, Malloy could take no more from his verbose opponent, and when play was at the Middlesbrough end, Clough ended up stretched out on the pitch after a great left hook from City's skipper. With everyone following the action at the other end, no one saw the incident – Malloy had no more trouble from Clough after that! City, however, lost 4-1.

## DON WAS NOT PLEASED!

Following the 4-1 defeat to Orient at Brisbane Road on 21 August 1971, which meant that City had conceded nine goals in their opening three matches, defender Don Murray was the subject of criticism in the local press. He confronted *South Wales Echo* football correspondent Peter Jackson in the *Echo* news-room, saying "It's a good job you're not manager, because if you were, then I'd be on the dole. Your eyes are in your \*\*\*\*!" Oddly enough, Don and Peter, and their wives, were all good friends and lived near each other in the Cyncoed area of Cardiff.

## NEARLY THE END OF WEMBLEY

Cardiff City's FA Cup Final appearance at Wembley in April 1927 was extremely close to becoming the last-ever event staged at the famous stadium. It was completed in 1923 for the British Empire Exhibition of 1924 and 1925, with a number of exhibition halls in close proximity to it. Several of these were demolished after the Exhibition, and the stadium itself went into liquidation a few months after the Bluebirds' successful appearance there. But businessman and entrepreneur Arthur Elvin, who had operated tobacconist and confectionery kiosks during the Exhibition, purchased Wembley from the liquidators and turned it into a going concern – but Cardiff City never returned there, nor yet to its successor.

## THE BLACKBOARD BOY

There was no public address system at Ninian Park until the late 1930s, nor were players numbered until 1939. Up to then, the match programme would list both teams from 1 to 22. Team changes referring to the numbers in the programme would be shown on a blackboard carried around the pitch by a boy before the kick-off. In the Bluebirds' archives is a photograph, taken at the end of April 1927 before the home game with Everton, of the FA Cup being carried around Ninian Park by the groundsman, followed by the boy with the blackboard.

# LONG TOUR

Cardiff City's longest-ever close-season tour was in the summer of 1968, when the club played fourteen matches across Oceania – in New Zealand, Australia and Tasmania. The tour party left London on 25 May, and didn't arrive home until 10 July having been away from Cardiff for nearly seven weeks. The dates and results of the matches while on tour were:

| Date | Opponents | Venue | Score |
|---|---|---|---|
| 28 May | New Caledonia | Noumea | 4-1 |
| 30 May | Auckland | Auckland | 3-0 |
| 1 June | Central League | Wellington | 2-3 |
| 3 June | Southern League | Christchurch | 2-0 |
| 5 June | New Zealand | Auckland | 3-0 |
| 9 June | Victoria | Melbourne | 1-1 |
| 10 June | Tasmania | Hobart | 5-1 |
| 15 June | North New South Wales | Newcastle | 2-0 |
| 16 June | New South Wales | Sydney | 1-1 |
| 19 June | Australian XI | Melbourne | 6-0 |
| 23 June | Queensland | Brisbane | 7-2 |
| 26 June | Australian XI | Sydney | 3-1 |
| 29 June | South Australia | Adelaide | 3-2 |
| 7 July | Western Australia | Perth | 6-1 |

# SIR HERBERT DID SIGN

Following Cardiff City's relegation from the old Division One in 1957, and consequent criticism of the board, club president and major shareholder Sir Herbert Merrett stated in a newspaper article that he had not wanted controversial Welsh international centre-forward Trevor Ford to join the club from Sunderland in December 1953 for a City record fee of £30,000. Merrett went on to state that the cheque to Sunderland was the only one that he had not signed personally during his time as a Bluebirds director. But Sir Herbert was mistaken – the directors' minutes of 10 December 1953 reveal that he, together with fellow-director Walter Riden, did sign the £30,000 cheque.

## A DISASTROUS START

Following their promotion from Division Two in May 1921, Cardiff City lost the opening six First Division games of the 1921/22 season and supporters were talking of an immediate relegation. But they recovered so well that they finished in fourth place, nine points behind Champions Liverpool. There were two points per win in those days, and if City had not made such a bad start, they would have been serious contenders for the League title.

## A EUROPEAN HEADED HAT-TRICK

Forward Sandy Allan, signed from Rhyl in March 1967, was a prolific scorer at reserve-team level, but never managed to establish himself in the first team. He did, however, create one City record when he headed a hat-trick in the European Cup Winners' Cup first round second-leg 5-1 home win over Mjondalen of Norway on 1 October 1969. He later played for Bristol Rovers.

## BLUEBIRDS FROM THE ORIENT

Two Far Eastern internationals have played for Cardiff City. In November 2002, 32-year-old Chinese international Fan Zhiyi (previously in British football with Crystal Palace and Dundee) was signed as a free agent. He was released at the end of that season. In December 2004, 25-year-old Japanese international Junichi Inamoto was signed on loan from West Bromwich Albion. He stayed until mid-March 2005.

## FARRELL'S MATCH TO REMEMBER

With three Second Division games remaining, Cardiff City retained their status with a 5-3 home win over Middlesbrough on 4 May 1966. It was a match remembered for an outstanding display by winger Greg Farrell, who single-handedly destroyed the opposition defence, with Middlesbrough relegated as a result of that game. But City's players must have thought that the season ended that night, because three days later they lost 9-0 at Preston!

## WELL PLAYED, DOCTOR

When Cardiff City played Swansea Town at the Vetch Field in the fourth qualifying round of the FA Cup on 29 November 1913, they included in their team a Cardiff medical practitioner. Dr J L McBean, an amateur who had previously been with Scottish club Queens Park before coming to Cardiff to set up in practice, played at left-back in what was his only first-team appearance. City lost 2-0, and he was back in his surgery on the Monday morning having to withstand friendly banter from those of his patients who were City fans.

## 'FELS NAPTHA'

The club produced a 'proper' match programme on a regular basis for the first time at the start of 1913/14 – a fold-over match day card had sufficed for the previous three seasons of Cardiff City's existence – and the firm that produced the new-style programme was the Imperial Printing Company of Frederick Street in Cardiff. Their managing director was Walter Parker, whose son Ivor had been one of City's first directors. Walter Parker himself joined the club's board in 1915, remaining a director for 24 years. He edited the programme for 19 years from 1913, under the pseudonym of 'Fels Naptha', which was a heavy-duty industrial soap used by his employees to clean their hands of printers' ink. Imperial Printing stopped producing the programme at the end of 1931/32, but the season-by-season bound volumes of their period as programme-printers (1913-1932) still exist, and are in the possession of Walter Parker's great-grandson Andrew Lewis, who is a Bluebirds season-ticket holder.

## NEARLY 60,000 FOR SWANSEA

The 1-0 home win over newly-promoted Swansea Town (as they were then called) attracted an all-ticket 57,510 attendance to Ninian Park on 27 August 1949. The actual number of tickets sold for the game was 60,855. The lesser figure was at the time a record for a League match at the ground.

## WEYMOUTH WOE

One of the most sensational FA Cup defeats in the club's history came in a Second Round tie on 11 December 1982, when the Bluebirds lost 2-3 at home to Weymouth. City were in a comfortable 2-0 lead by half time, with goals from Roger Gibbins and Jeff Hemmerman, but a series of disastrous errors saw City concede three second-half goals to their Southern League opponents.

## FARQUHARSON'S ENFORCED EXILE

The arrival in South Wales during 1920 of Cardiff City's long-serving goalkeeper Tom Farquharson, who was with the club from 1922 to 1935, had its origins in the civil and political unrest in Ireland at that time. The IRA's guerrilla war (1919-21) against British Forces over the question of Ireland's independence involved many Irish people who supported their aims. Farquharson was one of them, and was involved in fringe activities of a non-violent nature, such as running messages, hiding activists and reporting the movements of security forces. He and his friend Sean Lemass, who eventually became Taoiseach (Prime Minister) of the Irish Republic from 1959 to 1966, were arrested by British Forces for removing wanted posters displayed at St Stephen's Green and detained in Dublin's notorious Mountjoy Prison for questioning. Farquharson's father negotiated the release of his son through a friendly British Army major, but only on the condition that the 19-year-old Farquharson left Ireland immediately. So the tall teenager travelled in late 1920 to Monmouthshire's Sirhowy Valley, where he had contacts, and he worked as a carpenter. He had played Gaelic Football in Ireland, and its nearest equivalent in South Wales was Rugby Union. He turned out for Blackwood as a full-back, being a good handler of the ball. One day during the 1920/21 season, local football team Oakdale were short of a goalkeeper, and Farquharson volunteered his services, despite never previously having played the game. He proved such a success that Welsh League club Abertillery signed him, and it was from them that he joined Cardiff City in February 1922. He went on to make 509 League and Cup appearances for the Bluebirds, playing in two FA Cup Finals, and winning international honours for Ireland.

## DUTCH VISITORS

When the Festival of Britain was held in the summer months of 1951 to mark the country's steady emergence from the post-war austerity years, many Football League clubs played matches against continental sides to mark the event. So on 9 May 1951, Cardiff City played Dutch club PSV Eindhoven at Ninian Park. An attendance of 10,000 saw a 2-2 draw.

## A FOOTBALLERS' TRAIN

Following Cardiff City's 0-0 draw against Arsenal at Highbury on Boxing Day 1921, two open-coach charabancs were waiting outside the ground to take both teams to Paddington Station, where they caught the train to South Wales as they were playing each other in the return game at Ninian Park the following day. Also on the train for return fixtures were Newport County and Millwall, who had been playing at The Den, and Aberdare Athletic and Brentford who had faced each other at Griffin Park – it was an autograph hunter's delight.

## BEST-EVER START

Cardiff City's record from the first match of the 2006/07 season was nine wins, two draws and one defeat from the opening twelve League games. It was their best start since City entered League football in 1920. In contrast, the final nine matches of the season resulted in two draws and seven defeats – City's worst-ever finish in their League history.

## SEVENTY-SIX YEAR WAIT

When Bluebirds goalkeeper Neil Alexander gained his first senior Scotland cap, playing against Switzerland at Hampden Park on 1 March 2006 as a second-half substitute, he was the first Cardiff City player to represent Scotland at senior level for 76 years. Jimmy Nelson had won the last of his four caps in May 1930 against France in Paris.

## UNSUCCESSFUL AWAY TRIPS

Any intrepid supporters who had followed Cardiff City in all their away matches in Division Three (South) during 1932/33, would have gone to Clapton (now Leyton) Orient in City's final away match of that season hoping at last to see the Bluebirds win on their travels. Up to that time, City had not won away from home all season. It was no different at Orient – the Bluebirds lost 3-0. It was a similar situation near the end of the 1972/73 season in Division Two. City went to Millwall still looking for their first away win, but it was a 1-1 draw, and there was no away victory that season.

## A SERIOUS ILLNESS

At the start of 1921/22, following Cardiff City's promotion to the original First Division after their debut season in the Football League, the Bluebirds were without their Scottish international full-back Jimmy Blair, who had joined them from Sheffield Wednesday in November 1920. During the summer of 1921, Blair, who was still living in Sheffield, had contracted pneumonia. It was a serious matter, because in those days there were no antibiotics to combat such an illness. There were even worries that the player might not survive – but he recovered and was back in playing action by mid-September 1921.

## THIRTY SECONDS FROM £200,000!

When Nathan Blake was transferred from Cardiff City to Sheffield United for what seemed a modest £300,000 on 17 February 1994, Bluebirds chairman Rick Wright did the deal on the proviso that if the Yorkshire club stayed in the Premiership, then City would receive an extra £200,000. At the time of Blake's move, Sheffield United were in 21st place, and looked very likely to go down. In the end they almost saved themselves, but in their final game at Stamford Bridge, Chelsea beat them 3-2 with a goal 30 seconds from time. They were relegated just one point behind Ipswich Town, who had an inferior goal difference, and the Bluebirds missed out on £200,000!

## SUCCESSFUL LEAGUE OPENING

The very first Football League match to be played by Cardiff City was on 28 August 1920 in Division Two, at Stockport County, the club from whom secretary/manager Fred Stewart had joined the Bluebirds ten years earlier, and City won the game 5-2. The first League match at Ninian Park came two days later, when City drew 0-0 against Clapton (now Leyton) Orient in front of a 25,000 crowd.

## FORD INCREASED THE GATE

Welsh international centre-forward Trevor Ford made his home debut for Cardiff City against Middlesbrough on 12 December 1953, after his League record £30,000 transfer from Sunderland on 3 December, and following his first game for City in a 2-1 defeat at Sheffield Wednesday two days later. Ford scored the only goal of the game against Middlesbrough, when the Ninian Park attendance was 31,776 – over 10,000 up on the 21,284 who had seen the previous home match against Liverpool a fortnight earlier.

## NEAR-TRAGEDY FOR DWYER

Long-serving Phil Dwyer nearly lost his life whilst playing for Cardiff City. The Grangetown-born defender, who could also play in midfield and as a striker, was playing in City's Third Division away game at Gillingham on 8 November 1975 when he collided with an opposing defender. He was accidentally caught on the back of his head by the Gillingham player's knee, and fell unconscious to the ground. The impact caused him to swallow his tongue. He stopped breathing, and if it had not been for the prompt action of Bluebirds physio Ron Durham, Phil would have died. Ron used a corner-flagpole to clear Phil's airways, and he was taken to hospital in an ambulance that had driven onto the pitch. Unfortunately, a television news bulletin stated that he had died, the report heard in Cardiff by his wife and mother-in-law. They spent an extremely anxious period before discovering that he was all right. Phil, however, was tough – he was back in action for City seven days later against Colchester United at Ninian Park.

## KEENOR WANTED TRANSFER

Locally-born Welsh international Fred Keenor twice asked to leave Cardiff City during his nineteen-year career with the Bluebirds. In November 1921, he appeared before the directors and asked to be placed on the transfer list, having been left out of the team for several matches. His request was refused. And in January 1927, during the season in which he led City to that FA Cup Final win over Arsenal, he again asked for a move after being left out of the team, but nothing came of it.

## RECORD FA CUP WIN

An 8-0 home victory over Enfield in the first round of the FA Cup on 28 November 1931, watched by 6321, gave Cardiff City their biggest-ever win the competition. The Bluebirds beat Enfield twice more in the Cup – in December 1988 (4-1 in Round Two) and in November 1993 in Round One (0-0, 1-0). The Middlesex club eventually had their revenge when they beat City 1-0 at home in round one on 12 November 1994.

## POST-WAR GROUND IMPROVEMENTS

The main gates and white wall fronting Ninian Park on Sloper Road were built in the summer of 1947 following Cardiff City's Third Division (South) Championship success. The scheme was part of major ground improvements that included the building of a new terraced standing enclosure in front of the main stand.

## LEN'S INTERNATIONAL SHIRTS

When Cardiff City played Thames at Ninian Park in Division Three (South) on 6 February 1932, the East Londoners included former Bluebirds and Wales forward Len Davies. Because Thames had to change from their usual blue shirts, Len supplied his side with ten of his Welsh international shirts (not numbered in those days). The red shirts of Wales did not prove successful for Len and his colleagues – City beat them 9-2!

## FATHERS AND SONS

Only two pairs of fathers and sons have played League football for Cardiff City since the club entered the League in 1920. Jimmy Blair was an outstanding Scottish international full-back with the Bluebirds from 1920 to 1926. His younger son Doug was a highly-talented inside-forward, left-winger or half-back who was with City from 1947 to 1954. Cardiff-born forward John Toshack was with City from 1965 to 1970. His eldest son Cameron, also a forward, made four League appearances for the Bluebirds in February 1991.

## AND THE RAINS CAME DOWN

As the players came onto the pitch before the start of the Cardiff v Millwall match at Ninian Park on 4 November 1967, torrential rain had been falling for half an hour. City skipper Brian Harris borrowed an umbrella from long-time supporter Beryl Taylor, who always stood next to the players' tunnel behind the dug-out, and held it above his head. The referee – Arthur Jones of Ormskirk – took little notice, and commenced the match. It was abandoned at 0-0 after 31 minutes.

## GET OUT, AND STAY OUT!

Inside-forward Jimmy Gill joined Cardiff City from Sheffield Wednesday in July 1920 following Wednesday's relegation from Division One. He was followed to Ninian Park in mid-November 1920 by Wednesday's Scottish international left-back Jimmy Blair, and both proved to be great signings for the Bluebirds – but they both had an extremely hostile reception from home fans when City were 1-0 winners at Hillsborough on 4 December 1920. When Wednesday came to Cardiff for the return match seven days later, both players decided to pay a friendly visit on the morning of the game to see their former team-mates at the Grand Hotel in Cardiff's Westgate Street. A Wednesday director spotted them, and angrily told them to get out and stay out, and not to have anything to do with his players! That afternoon both Gill and Blair played a major part in another 1-0 win for City.

## CHEERING FOR THE WRONG TEAM

A number of Welshmen, who had emigrated to Watford several years earlier to find work, were amongst the 12,000 Vicarage Road crowd on 4 October 1936 to support City. Not having watched the Bluebirds for several seasons, they were obviously confused by the fact that Watford played in blue and Cardiff had changed to red. They kept cheering the wrong team, and were delighted with the 2-0 result - until they were put right at the final whistle by amused home fans, who pointed out that City had actually lost!

## THREE COUNTRIES, THREE CUP MEDALS

Two Cardiff City players – Tom Sloan and Tom Watson – both gained Cup Winners' medals from three different countries during their careers. In 1927 they won FA Cup and Welsh Cup winners' medals with Cardiff City, and after leaving the club in 1929, they both won Irish Cup Winners' medals with Linfield.

## HORSE FOR SALE

The following paragraph appeared in Cardiff City's match-programme early in the 1925/26 season... 'Horse For Sale – the directors have decided to purchase an electric mower and roller for the Ninian Park playing pitch. This will mean the disposal of the horse that has been assisting the groundsman with the present cutter and roller. Does anyone want a serviceable horse cheap? If so, write to our Secretary/Manager Mr Fred Stewart. We believe that those who have been looking after the horse will miss it very much. But, such is life, the best of friends must part.'

## CONSECUTIVE HAT-TRICKS

Only one Cardiff City player has scored hat-tricks for the club in two consecutive matches. On 18 January 1921, Len Davies scored four in a 7-1 home win over Newport County in the Welsh Cup. Three days later, he scored another three in the 6-3 First Division home win against Bradford City.

## CHARLIE THE COUNCILLOR

City skipper Charlie Brittan played for the club in a 2-1 win at Millwall in the First Division of the Southern League on 1 November 1919. Back in Cardiff, it was the day of local elections for the City Council. Brittan was a candidate for the Riverside Ward, having canvassed for the previous few months, and City's directors had allowed him to display posters for his candidature at Ninian Park on match days. Brittan was duly elected, and a large crowd was at Cardiff General Station on the team's return that Saturday evening to celebrate City's victory and Brittan's election as a Councillor. He kept his seat on the Council until his departure from Cardiff in 1924, when he retired from football and moved to Birmingham for business reasons.

## HIGHEST ATTENDANCES

Cardiff City's highest attendance for a first-team match at Ninian Park was the 57,893 who saw the Bluebirds draw 0-0 with eventual League Champions Arsenal on 22 April 1953, but the highest-ever attendance at the ground came on 17 October 1959, when Wales played England in the Home International Championship in front of 62,634.

## YOUNGEST-EVER BLUEBIRD

Midfield player Aaron Ramsey became the youngest-ever player to appear for Cardiff City in League football when he came on as substitute just before the end of the Championship match against Hull City at Ninian Park on 28 April 2007. Aaron, born on Boxing Day 1990, was 16 years and 123 days old at the time of his debut, beating the previous Bluebirds record set by John Toshack on 13 November 1965 against Leyton Orient. Toshack was 113 days older than Ramsey when the current Wales manager made his League debut, also as substitute. Former long-serving Bluebirds and Wales full-back Ronnie Stitfall was fourteen when he played for City in the early years of the 1939-45 war. That was in regional league wartime football, and was not counted in official Football League records.

## THE FA CUP IN SCOTLAND

In the late twenties and early thirties, the FA Cup winners would travel north of the border to meet the Scottish Cup winners in a friendly challenge match. The Bluebirds therefore met Celtic in Glasgow on 3 October 1927, losing 4-1 in front of an 8000 attendance at Celtic Park. Before the kick-off, both teams were photographed, together with their respective trophies.

## LONG-SERVING BLUEBIRDS MEDICAL OFFICERS

Scottish-born Dr Alex Brownlee, who became Medical Superintendent of Glan Ely Hospital, was a Cardiff City director and club Medical Officer from 1911 until he died in May 1951 – a period of 40 years. Merthyr-born Dr Leslie Hamilton was appointed the club's Medical Officer in 1965 and was connected with the Bluebirds until he died in 2000 – a period of 35 years.

## WORK PERMIT REFUSED

Cardiff City's first attempt to sign a foreign player came in the summer of 1928. The club had been on a three-match tour to Denmark in May of that year, and had been impressed by the ability of forward Creutz Jensen who had played against them for an Odense combined side. The Bluebirds actually signed Jensen, but the Ministry of Labour refused him a work permit.

## THREE KEEPERS IN ONE GAME

The Bluebirds used seven players in goal during the course of their 1982/83 promotion from Division Three – triallist Steve Humphreys (ex-Doncaster Rovers), Martin Thomas (on loan from Bristol Rovers), Andy Dibble, Jim Brown (on loan from Sheffield United), and Eric Steele (on loan from Watford) being the five established goalies. The other two were outfield players – Phil Dwyer and Linden Jones, who both went in goal at various times during the 4-2 defeat at Bradford City on 16 February 1983, when Andy Dibble had to go off because of injury.

## DEAF AND DUMB

In August 1924, Cardiff City signed James McLean from Belfast club Barn Athletic. McLean was deaf and dumb, but seemed to have no problems on the pitch, as his senses appeared to indicate to him the relative positions of his team-mates and when the referee had blown his whistle. He did not, however, make any first-team appearances, and was released at the end of the season.

## 1956/57/58 – AN FA CUP TREBLE AGAINST LEEDS

In the third round of the FA Cup on 7 January 1956, Cardiff City beat Leeds United 2-1 at Elland Road. A year later, on 5 January 1957 in round three, they again beat Leeds 2-1 at Elland Road. And twelve months after that, on 4 January 1958, they won 2-1 at Leeds in round three for the third consecutive year. The odds against that situation happening were 1,000,000 to 1!

## ALLISON'S CHAMPAGNE

Following City's 1-0 win at Crystal Palace in front of 25,863 on 10 April 1976, with both sides chasing promotion from Division Three, Palace's manager Malcolm Allison forecast that City would not get that kind of attendance for the battle with leaders Hereford United at Ninian Park four days later. He was right – City, who won 2-0, attracted 35,459, and the club sent Allison six bottles of his favourite champagne!

## TWO MANAGERIAL SPELLS

Four men have been managers of Cardiff City in two separate spells. Cyril Spiers was in charge from 20 April 1939 to 7 June 1946, and from 1 December 1947 to 10 May 1954. Len Ashurst was manager from 3 March 1982 to 4 March 1984, and from 31 August 1989 to 28 May 1991. Frank Burrows was manager from 21 May 1986 to 28 August 1989, and from 16 February 1998 to 31 January 2000. Eddie May was in charge from 11 July 1991 to 28 November 1994, and from 30 March 1995 to 31 May the same year.

## VOTED OUT

In early October 1977, a simmering disagreement in the boardroom culminated in Cardiff City's chairman Stefan Terlezski being voted out of his position by his fellow directors over the question of fans' identity cards, the introduction of which was supported by Mr Terlezski but opposed by the other directors. It was one of a number of issues on which they did not agree. Two months later, at an Extraordinary General Meeting of shareholders, the Cardiff hotelier was voted off the board. His successor as Chairman in late November 1977 was Bob Grogan, managing director of the Newcastle-based civil engineering firm Kenton Utilities. Mr Terlezski, who later became MP for Cardiff West, subsequently sued Mr Grogan for libel, and was awarded £4000 in damages by a Cardiff Crown Court jury.

## INTERNATIONAL FIRST

On 6 March 1911, Ninian Park staged its first-ever international match when Wales drew 2-2 against Scotland in the Home International Championship. It was the first season of the ground's existence, and a record 17,500 were packed in. For Scotland's wing-half Peter McWilliam, an outstanding player with Newcastle United, it was a fateful occasion. He fell and cut his knee on a piece of glass that had worked its way to the surface of what had been part of a rubbish tip several years earlier. As a result of the injury, McWilliam never played again. He later became manager of Tottenham and had many exciting tussles with Cardiff City during the 1920s.

## UP-MARKET PROPERTY FOR FORD

When Welsh international centre-forward Trevor Ford was transferred from Sunderland to Cardiff City in December 1953, he and his family lived with relatives in his home town of Swansea for a couple of months before City bought a house for him to rent in Earls Court Road, Cyncoed, Cardiff. The club paid £3750 for the semi-detached property, and rented it to Ford for £3.10 shillings (£3.50p) per week. Properties in that area now cost in the region of £375,000 – one hundred times the price of 1954.

## MATCH VOID

Following Cardiff City's Welsh Cup Final first leg draw against Hereford United at Ninian Park on 29 April 1976, which ended 2-2, it was discovered that Hereford midfielder Peter Spiring was ineligible for the game. He had been signed by them from Luton Town, but not registered with the FA of Wales at least fourteen days before the game, as per the rule. City would have been within their rights to file an objection and have Hereford removed from the competition. But the Bluebirds were content to let the FAW declare the match void, and played again. The rematch took place at Edgar Street, ending in a 3-3 draw, and City won the second leg 3-2.

## HARDY'S LACK OF INTERNATIONAL RECOGNITION

Bedlington-born half-back Billy Hardy, a Cardiff City player from 1911 to 1932, was described during the 1920s as the finest player in his position throughout the four Home Nations. But he never played for England, because the Football Association was unwilling to select any player from a club outside their jurisdiction in case they suffered the indignity of being refused his services. Hardy was, however, selected by the Football League for their 9-1 victory over the Irish League at Newcastle on 21 September 1927. Years later, Hardy described his lack of recognition by his country as "a small price to pay for being part of a very good Cardiff City side".

## COVERING THE POPULAR BANK

A major building project took place at Ninian Park in the 1958 close season, with the rear section of the open Popular Bank being stepped in concrete and covered with a large roof that extended the length of the pitch. The structural work was carried out by Connies and Meaden of Dumballs Road, who had built the Grange End covered terrace thirty years earlier. For two years, the roof remained a plain white, but on City's promotion to Division One in 1960, an ad for Captain Morgan Rum was painted on. It remained there for 42 years, changing colour in that period due to the weather and chemical changes in the paint.

## FAMOUS GUEST PLAYERS

During the 1939-45 War, clubs playing in regional league competitions were allowed to use guest players – usually servicemen in the Armed Forces who were stationed nearby. Four of League football's greatest names played on various occasions for Cardiff City during that period – Raich Carter (Sunderland and England), Bill Shankly (Preston and Scotland), Cliff Britton (Everton and England) and Johnny Carey (Manchester United).

## FA CUP REGULARS

As at 2007, Cardiff City had not reached the sixth round of the FA Cup since winning the trophy in 1927. But during the 1920s, no club played more FA Cup matches than the Bluebirds. From 1919/20, when they were in the Southern League, to 1929/30, City took part in 51 FA Cup ties!

## THE END OF THE OLD GRANGE END

During the course of the 1977/78 season, the Grange End roof and terracing, built in 1928 to accommodate 18,000 standing spectators, was deemed to be unsafe by structural engineers. The roof and terracing were therefore demolished and replaced by a smaller uncovered concrete terrace, which remained without a roof until 2001.

## A VISIT TO MARKS & SPENCER

Following the Bluebirds' fourth round FA Cup replay at Roker Park on 14 February 1972, which finished level at 1-1 after extra time, the tie had to go to a second replay, as was the rule in those days. It was arranged that it would take place two days later at Manchester City's Maine Road ground. City therefore stayed in the north, having expected to be away for just two days. It turned into a four-day trip, and the players and management had to go on a shopping expedition after reaching Manchester to buy shirts and underwear from Marks & Spencer, as they had not brought enough necessaries with them.

## LAST BLUEBIRDS AMATEUR FIRST-TEAMER

Llandudno-born Alan McIntosh was the last amateur player to appear in a League match for Cardiff City. A Welsh amateur international with his home-town club, McIntosh was a student teacher based in Cardiff, and played his first two League games for the Bluebirds as an amateur in February 1962. He appeared in the First Division game at Nottingham Forest on 17 February and at home to Manchester City a week later, signing professional in June 1962.

## HOME ATTENDANCES OF OVER 50,000

| Att | Opponents | Date |
| --- | --- | --- |
| 50,000 | Chelsea (FA Cup) | 5 March 1921 |
| 56,000* | Tottenham Hotspur (Division One) | 27 August 1921 |
| 50,470 | Nottingham Forest (FA Cup) | 18 February 1922 |
| 51,000 | Tottenham Hotspur (FA Cup) | 4 March 1922 |
| 50,000 | Tottenham Hotspur (Division One) | 2 September 1922 |
| 54,000 | Tottenham Hotspur (FA Cup) | 24 February 1923 |
| 50,000 | Sheffield United (Division One) | 26 December 1923 |
| 50,000 | Bristol City (FA Cup) | 23 February 1924 |
| 50,000 | Manchester City (FA Cup) | 10 March 1924 |
| 50,272 | Leicester City (FA Cup) | 7 March 1925 |
| 51,626 | Bristol City (Division 3 South) | 7 April 1947 |
| 56,018 | Tottenham Hotspur (Division 2) | 9 October 1948 |
| 57,510 | Swansea Town (Division 2) | 27 August 1949 |
| 51,000 | Leeds United (Division 2) | 3 May 1952 |
| 51,512 | Middlesbrough (Division 1) | 3 September 1952 |
| 52,202 | Newcastle United (Division 1) | 27 December 1952 |
| 57,893 | Arsenal (Division 1) | 22 April 1953 |
| 50,967 | West Bromwich Albion (Division 1) | 10 April 1954 |
| 55,000 | Aston Villa (Division 2) | 16 April 1960 |
| 55,136 | Arsenal (FA Cup) | 4 January 1969 |

*\* estimated attendance as spectators broke in after turnstiles were closed on just over 50,000*

## SUMMER JOBS

Despite the removal of League football's maximum wage in 1961, Cardiff City players were not overpaid. In fact, they had to accept a pay cut at the end of 1961/62 after the Bluebirds were relegated from Division One. Several of the players then found summer jobs, spending a month working for Cardiff Corporation, cutting the grass at Cathays Cemetery and generally keeping the area tidy.

## THE WRIGHT WAY

In March 1991, with Cardiff City struggling financially under chairman Tony Clemo, who had been in charge since 1986, a benefactor appeared in self-made businessman Rick Wright, who operated the Barry Island Majestic Holiday Centre. A former army frogman and commercial diver, Wright put an initial £30,000 into Cardiff City to help pay wages. He then funded the signings of Ken De Mange on loan from Hull City, Phil Heath of Oxford United, and loan signing Kevin MacDonald of Coventry City. Wright continued to help the club, becoming chairman at the end of 1991/92. The Bluebirds looked to be on their way to better fortunes by the end of 1992/93, when they won the Third Division Championship and the Welsh Cup, attracting good crowds during the later part of the season. Wright had some good ideas, including an admission structure based on the club's League position. But he then withdrew his financial support, as he had stated he would earlier in the season, expecting others to come in and take financial control of the club. He stayed as chairman until July 1995, with various groups promising takeovers that did not come about. As a consequence, City struggled financially in the mid-to-late 1990s.

## ANOTHER NELSON FA CUP MEDAL

Cardiff City's Scottish international full-back Jimmy Nelson won two FA Cup medals with Cardiff City – against Sheffield United, when the Bluebirds lost 1-0 in 1925, and against Arsenal when they won 1-0 in 1927. Following his move to Newcastle United in the summer of 1930, he led the north-east club to their 1932 victory over Arsenal when Newcastle were 2-1 winners.

## COSTLY APPEARANCE!

Goalkeeper Roger 'Roy' Ashton made just one League appearance for Cardiff City after being signed by the club in April 1948 following his earlier release by Wrexham. He played for City at Barnsley in a 2-1 defeat on 1 May 1948, but although he was registered with the Football League, the club had not obtained special permission to include him after the late-March transfer deadline, so City were fined five guineas by the League's Management Committee.

## HALF-CENTURY FOR KEENOR

Roath-born Welsh international Fred Keenor played for Cardiff City from 1912 until 1931, apart from three years when he served in the First World War. Although he played 369 League games for the Bluebirds, his first-team total was 505, which included 61 matches in the Southern League, 42 in the FA Cup, 1 in the FA Charity Shield and 32 in the Welsh Cup. After leaving City in May 1931, he spent four seasons with Crewe Alexandra before becoming player/manager at Oswestry Town. He was then in the same role with Tunbridge Wells Rangers, also running a shop and poultry farm while in Kent. He eventually returned to live in Cardiff in 1958, and became a storeman with Cardiff Corporation's Building Department. He died in a Cardiff residential home at the age of 78 in November 1972.

## KEEPING THEIR WORD

Billy Hardy (1911-32) and Len Davies (1919-31) were both loyal players with Cardiff City, and under League rules were entitled to cash benefits for every five years of service. But towards the end of their Bluebirds career, City simply could not afford to pay them their due benefits. Towards the end of the 1930s, the club's finances improved enough to enable them to fulfil their commitment to each player. On 29 April 1937, Cardiff City Present played Cardiff City Past, with Len Davies taking the gate receipts. Two seasons later, on 2 May 1939, Cardiff City played Fulham in a friendly, and Billy Hardy was given the proceeds.

# IRISH MISTAKE

Cardiff City full-back Jimmy Nelson, who had joined the Bluebirds from Belfast club Crusaders in the summer of 1921, was selected for Ireland during the 1923/24 season. The only problem was that he had no Irish connection apart from playing there. City had to tell the Irish FA that he was ineligible because a player then had to be born in a country to play for its national side. Nelson was born in Greenock, Scotland, and his father had gone with his family to Belfast from there in the early 1900s to work in the Harland and Woolf Shipyard. All the family were Scottish, and Nelson duly played for Scotland whilst with City. In fact, when he gained his first cap in February 1925 against Wales at Hearts' Tynecastle Park, it was the first time that he had ever played a match in his native country.

# RECORD-BREAKER COLLINS

In May 2004, Cardiff City's Newport-born defender James Collins created a Welsh international record. His appearance for Wales against Norway meant that he had become the first Welsh player to have been capped at every possible level for his country – schoolboy, various youth levels, under-21, 'B', and senior level.

# GOALSCORING DUO

Cardiff-born John Toshack and Bristolian Brian Clark formed a lethal goal-scoring partnership for Cardiff City in the late 1960s. They first played in the same City line-up on 3 February 1968 in a 4-3 win at Derby County, less than 24 hours after Clark had been signed from Huddersfield Town. Their final appearance together was on 4 November 1970, away to Nantes in the second leg of the European Cup Winners' Cup second round, and both scored in City's 2-1 win. Five days later, Toshack was transferred to Liverpool for £110,000. During the two previous seasons, the two had scored exactly 100 goals between them. In 1968/69, Clark scored 17 League and two Cup goals while Toshack netted 22 League and nine Cup goals (50 in total). In 1969/70, Clark hit 18 League goals and ten Cup goals while Toshack scored 17 League goals and five Cup goals (another 50 in total).

## TOP-SCORING WINGER

Peter Hooper joined Cardiff City from Bristol Rovers in the summer of 1962 following the Bluebirds' relegation from Division One. Left-winger Hooper spent only the one season at Ninian Park, but left his mark by becoming top scorer with 22 League goals, plus another two in Cup matches. He then joined Bristol City, having become the only winger in City's history to have been their leading League scorer in a season.

## BLUEBIRDS' INTERNATIONAL CAPTAINS

When Wales played Scotland at Ninian Park on 16 February 1924, both sides were captained by Cardiff City players – Fred Keenor (Wales) and Jimmy Blair (Scotland). In those days, international players were only supplied with shirts, and were required to bring with them club shorts and socks, so both players wore the blue socks of Cardiff City. Wales won 2-0, and the two captains went home together after the game.

## LATE FINISH

The 1946/47 season was badly disrupted by the severe winter of that year. Cardiff City did not play their final match in Division Three (South) until 7 June 1947, when they defeated Leyton Orient 1-0 at Ninian Park. At the end of the game, skipper Fred Stansfield was presented with the Championship Shield of Division Three (South), which City had won comfortably.

## PINCHING OURSELVES

Bluebirds' legendary goalscorer Brian Clark remains convinced that, on the night of the 1-0 win against the even more legendary Real Madrid on 10 March 1971, there were more present at Ninian Park for the European Cup Winners' Cup quarter-final first-leg tie than the official attendance of 47,500. He could well have been right, because a considerable number were able to 'pinch in' at the rear of the Popular Bank near the railway line.

## EUROPEAN REGULARS

During the mid 1960s and early 1970s, no British club appeared in European competition more often than Cardiff City. From September 1964 to October 1975, the Bluebirds played in 35 European Cup Winners' Cup matches, qualifying by being winners of the Welsh Senior Cup. City twice reached the quarter-finals and once reached the semi-finals. They also played in a further 14 Cup Winners' Cup matches between August 1976 and September 1994, a total of 49 matches over a thirty-year period.

## POLITICAL PROBLEMS

Following Cardiff City's promotion to Division One at the end of 1959/60, they were due to play several matches in East Germany. But because of the U2 spy-plane incident, when a high-level USA reconnaissance aircraft was shot down by a Soviet missile, the East German border was closed to westerners. City still went to Switzerland, where they had been due to start their tour, and met up with Sunderland, who were also due to play matches in East Germany. So the two clubs played one match against each other, a 0-0 draw in Berne, before returning home.

## GETTING OUT OF GAOL

On the night before their European Cup Winners' Cup first round second-leg tie against the Belgian club Standard Liège on 20 October 1965, the Bluebirds had a few problems. Three of the squad – George Johnston, Bernard Lewis, and 16-year-old John Toshack, who was an apprentice professional – went out for a walk in Liège, stopping for a sandwich and a soft drink at a nearby café. Johnston and Lewis argued with the waiter over the bill, and in their anger hurled a chair from the café into a nearby river. A passer-by saw the whole incident and called the police, resulting in the three players being detained in the local prison until 2am,when manager Jimmy Scoular, who had been summoned from the team's hotel, was able to persuade the authorities to release them. The volatile Scot was less than happy with his three players! City lost the game 1-0.

## A LONG-AWAITED EXTENSION

Over the course of the 1972/73 season, the centre section of the main stand, originally built in 1938, was finally extended with wing stands on either side. The project involved reducing the depth of the main stand enclosure and lowering the ground's capacity. The new scheme was intended to be finished shortly after the Second World War, but for various reasons its completion took 35 years from the date that the original centre section was built.

## 1946/47/48 – CLARKE'S TRIPLE ACHIEVEMENT

Outside-left Roy Clarke played his final game for Cardiff City on 17 May 1947 at Exeter City in Division Three (South). He was then transferred to Manchester City, who were in Division Two, and played in their final match of the season on 14 June of the same year, as they completed their promotion with a 5-1 win over Newport County. His next match was a First Division game for Manchester City against Wolves on 23 August 1947 – three successive appearances in three different divisions!

## WOODY'S FORTY-YARDER

Midfield player Bobby Woodruff, who joined Cardiff City from Crystal Palace in November 1969, was well known for his long throw-ins, often over a distance of forty yards. But he could also score long-range goals, as he did on 6 October 1973 in the match against Aston Villa at Villa Park, when he headed in from forty yards to open the scoring after five minutes. Unfortunately, it was into his own net, and City lost 5-0!

## PAY UP FOR THE BALL

It is usually the custom for any player scoring a hat-trick to be given the match ball, but when Reading's Trevor Senior scored all three in his side's Third Division 3-1 victory at Ninian Park on 31 August 1985, he was told by cash-strapped City that he could have the ball – but only if he paid £40 for it!

## BEST DEFENCE, BUT RELEGATED!

No team had a better defensive record in Division One than Cardiff City in 1928/29 – just 59 goals conceded in their 42 matches. Unfortunately, the Bluebirds could score only 43, and went down, finishing in bottom place. Seven of their goals had come in the opening home match against Burnley when they had won 7-0. City lost eight of their matches by the odd goal, and drew thirteen. Another eight goals over those 21 matches would have kept them up.

## ON THE GIRDERS

A record crowd of 42,000 attended the Cardiff City v Coventry City match on 27 December 1920, a considerable number of them on the girders and roof-supports of the then-uncompleted Canton Stand. Construction had begun in July 1920 and would not be finished until July 1921. The new stand was built out of alignment with the pitch as the intention was to move the playing area ten yards nearer to Sloper Road and to build a 9000-capacity modern main stand to replace the wooden structure built in 1910. That scheme was shelved because of lack of finance, and the Canton Stand (now known as the Spar Family Stand) is still out of alignment with the pitch when viewed from the Grange End.

## AND THE STAND WENT UP IN FLAMES

At 3.45am on 18 January 1937, Police Constable Bradshaw, on duty on the corner of Sloper Road and Leckwith Road near Ninian Park railway station, saw smoke and flames rising from Ninian Park's wooden main stand, built in November 1910. Despite the Fire Brigade being in prompt attendance, the stand was completely destroyed, together with the players' kit. The club's pedigree Airedale watchdog Jack died in the fire, as did one of the club's cats. The survivor was Trixie who, ten years earlier, had gone with City as a kitten to Wembley after being found on the Royal Birkdale golf course at Southport while the players were in training for their FA Cup fifth round match at Bolton.

## SORRY – YOU MISSED IT!

Any spectators who came in a minute after the kick-off for three particular Cardiff City matches would have found the Bluebirds one down. On 27 October 1967, in Division Two at Boothferry Park, Hull City's Ken Wagstaff scored after 13 seconds, but Cardiff recovered to win 2-1 through Bobby Brown and Ronnie Bird. On 3 September 1955, in Division One at Ninian Park, Wolves winger Johnny Hancocks netted in 15 seconds – Wolves went on to win 9-1! And on 3 February 1974 at Ninian Park, Aston Villa's Ray Graydon scored in 43 seconds of a Second Division match – it was the only goal of the game.

## STEADY RISE

Cardiff City's average home League attendances have shown a steady increase over the last ten years:

| Season | Average |
| --- | --- |
| 1996/97 | 3594 |
| 1997/98 | 3574 |
| 1998/99 | 7131 |
| 1999/2000 | 6895 |
| 2000/01 | 7962 |
| 2001/02 | 12,522 |
| 2002/03 | 13,049 |
| 2003/04 | 15,569 |
| 2004/05 | 13,029 |
| 2005/06 | 11,802 |
| 2006/07 | 15,244 |

## HONEYMOON LIMOUSINE FOR BLUEBIRDS

When Cardiff City went to Coventry City for a Third Division (South) fixture on 6 April 1935, the team travelled from Cardiff in several limousines, one of which had recently been used by the Duke and Duchess of Kent on their honeymoon. But the luxurious transport was of no assistance to the Bluebirds, who lost 2-0.

## TEN-SEATER AIRCRAFT

In the late 1970s, Cardiff City's parent company – Kenton Utilities of Newcastle – transferred ownership of a ten-seater aircraft to the club for tax purposes. At that time, teams could name just one substitute, so it was a case of a twelve-man squad for matches. *South Wales Echo* football correspondent Joe Lovejoy wrote a tongue-in-cheek story that if City used the aircraft for away matches, then two players would have to find alternative methods of travel. Meanwhile *Echo* cartoonist Gren showed City's aircraft taking off with two players sitting on either wing – Kenton Utilities were not amused!

## TRAGIC LOSS

Former Wales Schools international Trevor 'Slogger' Williams was a young half-back who became a professional with Cardiff City in 1936/37. Barry-born Williams, regarded as one of City's most promising youngsters, was a regular in the reserves during the first few months of 1937/38. He played for the second team on Saturday 2 October 1937, but on the following Wednesday, when he reported for training, 18-year-old Williams was taken ill with appendicitis, and was rushed to Cardiff Royal Infirmary. He underwent an immediate operation, but there were complications and he died two days later. His funeral took place in Barry on 13 October, and was attended by all the club's players and staff.

## FIRST OVERSEAS TOUR

The Bluebirds travelled abroad for the first time in May 1924, when the newly-formed Czechoslovakian FA sponsored a five-match tour to Czechoslovakia, Austria and Germany. They travelled by train and cross-channel ferry, taking three days to arrive in Prague where they played two matches against Sparta Prague (a 2-3 defeat followed by a 3-2 victory). They then travelled to Austria for a 2-0 win against First Vienna, before moving on to Germany where they defeated Borussia of Berlin 2-0, finishing with a 2-2 draw against SV Hamburg. Forty-four years later, City were to meet SV Hamburg again – in the semi-final of the European Cup Winners' Cup.

# BADGES

It was not until 1958/59 that Cardiff City wore a badge on their shirts. Since then, they have always worn one, though it has taken different forms over the years. It has always shown either a bluebird, or the word itself. When City played in the 1925 and 1927 FA Cup Finals, however, they wore the City of Cardiff coat of arms by special permission of the Lord Mayor and City Corporation.

# POINTS STRUCK OFF

Cardiff City were deducted six points in Division Four during March 1992 because of Aldershot's resignation from the Football League. The Bluebirds had beaten them 2-1 at the Recreation Ground on 8 November 1991, with goals from Nathan Blake and Paul Millar, and 2-0 at Ninian Park on 20 March 1992, the goals coming from Blake and Carl Dale. The results were deleted from the record, and the three players lost their goals. The same situation applied to other clubs who had played Aldershot, and any players who had scored against them.

# AN ARSENAL TREBLE

Cardiff City defeated Arsenal on three consecutive Saturdays during the 1923/24 season. From 1919 to 1924, League clubs played home and away against the same opposition on consecutive weekends. On 19 January 1924, City were 2-1 winners at Highbury in Division One. The following weekend, the Bluebirds beat the Gunners 4-0 in the return match at Ninian Park. Finally, on 2 February, the two clubs again met at Ninian Park – this time in the FA Cup. Once again City came out on top, beating the London club 1-0.

# FIRST OVERSEAS VISITORS

The first continental club side to play at Ninian Park were Racing Club de Lens, who played a friendly on 6 October 1937 when Cardiff City defeated them 3-1. The match was arranged through Racing Club's trainer/coach Johnny Galbraith, who had been a Bluebirds defender from February 1931 until the end of 1934/35.

## MONTY ASKED FOR MONTY

The famous wartime soldier Field Marshal Viscount Montgomery of Alamein was in Cardiff on ceremonial duty on 31 October 1953. He attended the Cardiff City v Charlton Athletic match, and was introduced to both teams before the start. He was President of Portsmouth FC, and a keen football follower. After City's 5-0 win, he "ordered" his namesake and Bluebirds defender Stan Montgomery up to the boardroom for a photograph. Stan arrived, still in his playing kit, for a picture that he always displayed prominently at his Llanishen home for the rest of his life.

## THE FA CUP'S CARDIFF HOME

Following Cardiff City's victory over Arsenal in the 1927 Cup Final, the directors invited the National Museum of Wales to display the trophy during the period that City held it. But the offer was declined, and so the board resolved that the Cup would be kept in the possession of their chairman Walter Parker. It therefore resided at his Canton home in Talbot Street, though it was taken on numerous occasions to be exhibited for charity at various venues in Cardiff and throughout Wales. It also went to Ilfracombe and Bideford during the first few months of the 1927/28 season, when City played friendly matches at those North Devon venues.

## NUMBERS GAME

The start of the abandoned 1939/40 season saw Football League players numbered for the first time. Cardiff City wore 2 to 11, the goalkeeper being unnumbered as per the new regulation, in their opening Third Division (South) game, when they were 2-1 winners at Norwich City on 26 August 1939. But that match, plus City's next two games (a 1-0 win at Swindon four days later, followed by a 2-4 home defeat against Notts County on 2 September) were struck from the records, along with all other League results up to then, because of the outbreak of war on 3 September 1939. The League programme was immediately abandoned, and after various friendly fixtures in September/early-October, regional league competitions were started.

## UP THE HILL

Cardiff City's Welsh international Derek Tapscott, who was signed from Arsenal in September 1958, lived in Rhiwbina, and would often do some running near his home after training. In company with his fellow Welsh international, Bluebirds Alan Harrington and Colin Baker, who both lived near him, he would run up Caerphilly mountain to the summit. But before running down again, they would call into the Travellers' Rest for a half a shandy – those were the days!

## A DELICATE MATTER

*From Cardiff City's match programme, 13 November 1920*
'One matter that is very delicate to touch upon is the congestion of the board room on the occasion of a big match. Many friends of the club from near and far look in and partake of what hospitality the directors can offer - so far so good. The boardroom, however, is not a lounge, and those who come and go quickly will always be the most welcome. It must not be forgotten that the home directors owe a duty of hospitality to the visiting directors and this they are unable to fulfil under the conditions referred to.'

## THE BOSS MADE FA CUP HISTORY

Cardiff City's manager Jimmy Scoular (1964-73) was the first-ever player to appear for two clubs in the FA Cup during the same season. Scoular, who was from Livingston near Edinburgh, had been an apprentice foundry worker, but left home at the age of eighteen in 1943 to join the Royal Navy. He was stationed at HMS Dolphin – the submarine shore-base at Gosport in Hampshire. In the first half of 1945/46, Scoular was with Gosport Borough Athletic, for whom he played in the first qualifying round against Salisbury Corinthians, and in the second qualifying round against Newport, Isle of Wight. In December 1945, he was transferred to Portsmouth, for whom he played in the third round against Birmingham City. No one at the time appeared to question this, and years later Scoular said "No-one ever asked me at Portsmouth if I'd already played in the competition that season, and I never told them!"

## TRAINING GROUND

The Bluebirds have done the rounds of the area over the years when it comes to training grounds. They have used Corinthian Park (now a housing estate) off Llandaff Road, Coronation Park off Sloper Road, Guest Keen Nettlefold's sports ground (now a housing estate) which was on the corner of Sloper Road and Bessemer Road, Fitzalan High School off Broad Street, the University of Glamorgan sports ground at Treforest, and Barry Town's Jenner Park.

## BLUEBIRDS FILM ARCHIVE

The earliest film that exists of Cardiff City in action shows an FA Cup match against Tottenham Hotspur at Ninian Park in February 1923. There is also film of the Bluebirds' two FA Cup Finals (1925 and 1927) plus action from two other City FA Cup matches in 1926/27. From the 1930s, there is action from a Third Division (South) match against Luton Town at Ninian Park during September 1936, and the Moscow Dynamo match in November 1945 is well covered. From 1959 onwards, there is no shortage of historical film coverage.

## THREE OFF

Cardiff City once finished a League match with just eight players! On 28 December 1999, the Bluebirds were away to Cambridge United, and had Russell Perrett, Craig Middleton, and Lee Phillips all sent off for various offences. City held out for a 0-0 draw, with goalkeeper Jon Hallworth saving a penalty!

## BEST/WORST OPENING DAYS

The Bluebirds' best-ever result in an opening-day-of-the-season match was on 18 August 1951, when they defeated Leicester City 4-0 in a Second Division match at Ninian Park. Their worst-ever opening-day result was on 10 August 1968 in Division Two, when they lost 0-4 to Crystal Palace at Ninian Park.

# DEDICATED FANS

Cardiff City clinched promotion from the original Second Division with a game to spare at the end of their very first Football League season, when they defeated Wolverhampton Wanderers 1-0 at Ninian Park on 2 May 1921. Amongst the 40,000 gate were numerous miners from the Valleys, who could not afford both the rail fare and the admission price – so they walked more than 20 miles to Cardiff for the game. At least they were happy on the long journey back.

# ENGLAND REPRESENTATION

No Cardiff City player has yet represented England in a full international whilst still a Bluebirds player, but two City players have appeared for England 'B'. At the end of 1951/52, following City's promotion to Division One, the Football Association selected Wilf Grant and Charlie Rutter to play against France 'B' at Le Havre on 22 May 1952. The following season, Rutter was selected to play against Holland 'B' in Amsterdam, but had to miss out through injury. Gerry Hitchens played for England under-23s in their 3-0 victory against Denmark in Copenhagen on 26 September 1956 whilst a City player. He did play for England at senior level, but that was in 1960/61, four years after he had left the Bluebirds for Aston Villa. John Impey played for England Youth in 1973, and Cameron Jerome played for England under-21s in 2005/06 before his transfer to Birmingham City. Peter Whittingham has been an England under-21 international whilst with Cardiff City.

# EX-ENGLAND CAPTAINS

Two former England captains played for Cardiff City. In January 1929, the Bluebirds signed half-back Frank Moss from Aston Villa, but he played in only nine League matches before leaving to join Oldham Athletic at the end of 1928/29, following City's relegation from Division One. In September 1984, former Exeter City player/manager Gerry Francis (ex-Queens Park Rangers, Crystal Palace and Coventry City) joined the Bluebirds as a non-contract player, and appeared in seven League games before moving on to join Swansea City.

## ONE-MATCH WONDERS

At the end of the 2006/07 season these 65 players had appeared in just one Football League match for Cardiff City:

| *Name* | *Opponent* | *Venue* | *Date* |
| --- | --- | --- | --- |
| Len Abram | Clapton Orient | H | 30/08/21 |
| Ernie Anderson | Oldham Athletic | A | 17/09/21 |
| Roy Ashton | Barnsley | A | 01/05/48 |
| John Bartlett | Queen's Park Rangers | A | 21/10/33 |
| Ralph Blakemore | Bury | H | 02/05/31 |
| Mirko Bolesan | Scunthorpe United | H | 31/10/96 |
| Alistair Brack | Middlesbrough | H | 01/09/62 |
| Dennis Callan | Huddersfield Town | H | 24/09/55 |
| Hugh Campbell | Bristol City | A | 01/05/37 |
| Ernie Carless | Exeter City | H | 05/11/32 |
| Jack Court | Crystal Palace | H | 25/03/39 |
| Jim Davies | Aldershot | A | 03/12/38 |
| Rollo Evans | Aldershot | H | 04/02/33 |
| Trevor Evans | Northampton Town | A | 07/05/38 |
| Jim Finlay | Notts County | A | 05/02/38 |
| Alex Gilchrist | Bradford Park Avenue | A | 21/08/48 |
| Ben Graham | Bradford City | A | 07/05/94 |
| Wyn Griffiths | Newcastle United | H | 10/04/48 |
| Jim Harrison | Bristol Rovers | H | 15/04/38 |
| Graham Hogg | Bury | A | 19/03/49 |
| Matty Holmes | Aldershot | H | 25/03/89 |
| Ralph Horton | Bristol City | H | 03/12/32 |
| Mike Hughes | Sunderland | H | 22/04/59 |
| Steve Humphries | Wrexham | H | 28/08/82 |
| Alan Jones | Rotherham United | A | 21/04/58 |
| Charlie Jones | Stoke | H | 05/02/21 |
| George Latham | Blackburn Rovers | A | 02/01/22 |
| Jack Lewis | Bury | A | 21/03/25 |
| Kevin J. Lloyd | Notts County | A | 18/08/79 |
| Bobby McLaren | Luton Town | A | 18/03/50 |
| Ray McStay | Mansfield Town | H | 21/12/96 |
| Paul Marriott | Wrexham | H | 05/10/91 |

| Name | Opponent | Venue | Date |
|------|----------|-------|------|
| Ernie Marshall* | Notts County | H | 07/09/46 |
| Fred Mason | Sheffield United | H | 14/04/23 |
| Harry May | Leicester City | A | 21/01/50 |
| Alf Mayo | Bury | H | 02/05/31 |
| Curtis McDonald | Coventry City | A | 30/04/06 |
| Jim Melville | Tottenham Hotspur | A | 03/09/21 |
| Ross Menzies | Charlton Athletic | A | 01/02/58 |
| Jamie Michael | Mansfield | H | 21/12/96 |
| Don Mills | Barnsley | H | 07/04/51 |
| Paddy Moore | Charlton | A | 31/08/29 |
| Jerry Murphy | Arsenal | A | 06/04/28 |
| Pat Murphy | Leyton Orient | A | 08/01/66 |
| Joe Nibloe | Lincoln City | A | 13/11/48 |
| Griff Norman | Southampton | A | 22/09/51 |
| Harry Parfitt | Bolton | A | 06/02/54 |
| Gordon Pembery | Plymouth Argyle | A | 27/12/49 |
| Cliff Powell | Bury | H | 03/11/89 |
| Cecil Price | West Ham | A | 16/10/48 |
| Aaron Ramsey | Hull City | H | 28/04/07 |
| Len Richards | Luton Town | A | 29/10/32 |
| Andy Spring | Gillingham | A | 12/10/85 |
| Sid Taylor | Bristol Rovers | A | 22/04/35 |
| Billy Turnbull | Oldham | H | 28/04/23 |
| Lee Walker | Bradford City | A | 07/05/94 |
| Alan Walsh | Northampton Town | A | 28/03/92 |
| Phil Watkins | Portsmouth | A | 11/01/64 |
| Billy Watson | Coventry City | H | 15/11/47 |
| Tom Wilson | Oldham | A | 18/10/30 |
| Jack Winspear | Preston | A | 12/11/66 |
| Jonathan Woods | Brighton | H | 08/09/84 |
| Billy Woof | Wigan Athletic | H | 11/09/82 |
| Eddie Youds | Bolton | A | 20/01/89 |
| Peter Zois | Rotherham United | H | 24/02/98 |

*Ernie Marshall played in the opening three Football League games of the abandoned 1939/40 season, but these appearances did not count in the official records.*

# FAR AND WIDE

During World War Two, many Cardiff City players were in the Armed Forces. Meanwhile the club, playing in wartime regional competition, used locally-based young players in reserved occupations (miners, transport workers, dockers, etc.) as well as guest players, usually servicemen stationed at RAF St Athan or at nearby army bases, and who were professional players with other clubs. In late April 1944, a year before the end of the war in Europe, the whereabouts of City players in the forces were listed as follows:

*Serving Overseas*

HV Baker (RAF), G Ballsom (Army), R Bewley (Army), S Booth (RAF), J Butler (Army), R Calnan (Army), R Colbourn (Army), WJ Edwards (RAF), W Evans (RAF), SW Glass (RAF), T Grocrott (RAF), T Hardy (Navy), D Henry (Army), C Hill (Army), FA Jenkins (RAF), K Hollyman (Fleet Air Arm), W Lewis (Army), J Phelps (Navy), G Price (Army), R Pugh (Army), E Richards (Army), B Ross (Navy), R Shepherd (Army), J Steggles (RAF), W Sneddon (RAF), P Townsend (RAF), WT Willicomb (RAF).

*Died in Action*

R Anderson (RAF), L Evans (Royal Marines), J Stockford (Royal Navy), W Phillips (Royal Navy).

*Missing in Action*

S Shepherd (RAF)

*Wounded in Action*

J Cringan (Army), PJ Hart (Navy), JA Williams (RAF), J Allen (Army).

*Based in Britain*

R Anderson (Army), T Anderson (Army), W Brooks, G Conway (Navy), R Cameron, J Court (Royal Marines), A Cowley (RAF), J Daly (RAF), R Dare (RAF), I Davies (Army), T Davies, P Densham (RAF), K Devonshire, R Dunstan (Army), ET Edwards

(Army), M Gilcrist (Army), F Gregory (RAF), A Granville (RAF), G Gunn (Army), F Hall (RAF), M Halliwell (Army), V Hobbs (RAF), D Howell, I Hughes (RAF), D Hustwick (Army), ST Johns (Army), T Jones (Royal Marines), H Joy (RAF), E Marshall (Army), L McPhillips (RAF), R Meads (RAF), WJ Mitchell (Army), D Morgan (Army), G Morgan (Army), Glyn Morgan, Reg Morgan (Army), T Morris (RAF), J Myers, L Orphan (Army), L Parker (RAF), D Parry, H Pearson, D Pickwick (RAF), R Phillips (Fleet Air Arm), H Presdee (Army), C Prosser (Army), C Poley (Navy), N Rees (Army), W Rossitter (Army), W Russell, G Savin (Army), G Sergeant (RAF), W Scott, G Scammell (Navy), G Sparshott (Army), AE Stitfall (Navy), R Stitfall (Navy), R Sullivan (Army), AE Sykes, L Sweetman (Navy), A Williams (Army), TD Williams (Army), A Wright (RAF), R Vizard (Army).